ANNABEL KARMEL'S
FEEDING
YOUR
BABY & TODDLER

ANNABEL KARMEL'S
FEEDING
YOUR
BABY & TODDLER

The Complete Cookbook

DORLING KINDERSLEY

London • New York • Sydney • Moscow

www.dk.com

A DORLING KINDERSLEY BOOK

www.dk.com

Project Editor
Lorna Damms

Deputy Art Director
Carole Ash

Editor
Lorraine Turner

Managing Editors
Corinne Roberts &
Mary Ling

Art Editors
Carmel O'Neill & Emy Manby

Consultant Editor
(on child development)
Caroline Greene

Senior Art Editor
Carole Oliver

DTP Designer
Bridget Roseberry

Food Photography
Ian O'Leary

Production Manager
Maryann Rogers

Model Photography
Andy Crawford

Production Controller
Martin Croshaw

Home Economist
Janice Murfitt

Note on the nutritional breakdowns of recipes:
please note that all information is approximate and based on figures from food composition tables, not on direct analysis of made up dishes. Thus analyses should be used as a guide, not as guaranteed figures. As some ingredients are not specified by weight, an estimated weight has been used. No analyses have been provided for recipe variations. Analyses are per portion.

As many vitamins are destroyed when exposed to air or light, the guidelines on rich sources apply to dishes served immediately after preparation. Where recipes are frozen immediately, they will, in general, still provide a useful amount of the nutrients indicated. The wording "Rich source" has been based on both absolute values and values when compared to the energy (KCal) content of the recipe.

First published in Great Britain in 1999
by Dorling Kindersley Limited,
9 Henrietta Street, London WC2E 8PS

A CIP catalogue for this book is available
from the British Library.

ISBN 0 7513 0614 2

Reproduced in Italy by GRB
Printed and bound in China by L.Rex Printing Co., Ltd.

CONTENTS

4–6 MONTHS

A guide to successful weaning, with advice on introducing solids, and featuring a photographic gallery of first purées and 14 simple recipes.

6–9 MONTHS

Expert information on introducing new tastes and textures, followed by a gallery of more advanced purées and 27 recipes.

Introduction

When it comes to the health and happiness of their child, I think that all parents will agree that only the very best will do. I lost my first child, Natasha, at the heartbreakingly early age of 13 weeks after she contracted a viral infection. Though this illness was not diet-related, Natasha's loss made me even more determined to give my second child, Nicholas, the best possible start in life. It was Nicholas who gave me my first experience of coping with a fussy eater. Indeed, my interest in the whole subject of child nutrition was born out of my own frustrations with feeding a child who for a time would eat only a limited range of foods. Thus the strategies and solutions for common feeding problems that are presented in this book are based not only on current nutritional guidelines, but on experience and a deep conviction that food is one of the best forms of preventive medicine.

❖

At the time when diet is most crucial to health, we should not be reliant upon processed foods from jars and packets. After all, there is no great mystique to making baby food and there is nothing better for your child than home-cooked food made from fresh ingredients. Home cooking is an economical option and, as the recipes in this book show, it need not be time-consuming. There are many excellent purées that do not involve cooking and other recipes suitable for batch-cooking that enable a whole month's food supply to be prepared in just a couple of hours and then frozen. These homemade meals accustom babies to the natural variations in taste of freshly cooked food, and this helps them adapt to family meals and grow up to be less fussy eaters. So while parents are giving their baby the best nutritional start in life, they are also helping to guard against future feeding difficulties.

Unfortunately, for many children convenience and junk foods are a regular part of their diet: fewer and fewer families are sitting down to meals together. Instead, children are often raised on a depressingly familiar repertoire of processed, packaged foods and "TV dinners" – pizzas, chicken nuggets, chips and spaghetti hoops. It can seem that "real" food is only for adults, and that children have a special diet consisting of some of the poorest quality, most unhealthy food on offer. Yet parents are the ones in charge of what their children eat, and it is up to parents to give their children the opportunity to follow a varied, healthy diet.

❖

My three children, Nicholas, Lara and Scarlett, have been my constant inspiration over the years, but I am also grateful to all the babies and young children who have contributed to my research into nutrition and development, albeit unknowingly, and tested my new recipes. Children are exacting critics and while they are rarely interested in whether their food is healthy, they do care if it tastes good. Accordingly, the recipes in this book are designed to combine "child appeal" with sound nutritional principles.
I hope that many of them will be firm family favourites for years to come.

Annabel Karmel.

Early Nutrition

A BALANCED DIET is one that perfectly suits your growing child's needs. Breast milk or formula is an essential source of nourishment throughout the first year of your baby's life, but from the time you begin weaning him, you should work towards establishing a diet that provides the five essential nutrients: carbohydrate, vitamins, fat, minerals and protein. Remember that your child's needs are different from your own. The average adult is advised to follow a high-fibre, low-fat diet, but the under 5s need significantly more fat and concentrated sources of calories and nutrients to fuel their rapid growth during the early years.

Your baby's milk

Throughout his first 6 months, your baby is totally dependent on breast milk or formula for all his nutritional needs. Although you may have begun weaning your baby at 4 or 5 months, his initial solid intake is so small that these "real" foods are little more than a taste experience, and it is vital not to reduce milk feeds. Once your baby is 6 months old, you can introduce small quantities of cow's milk in cooking and with breakfast cereals. Once he reaches his first birthday, cow's milk can become his usual drink, but until then he needs the vitamins and iron found in breast milk or formula.

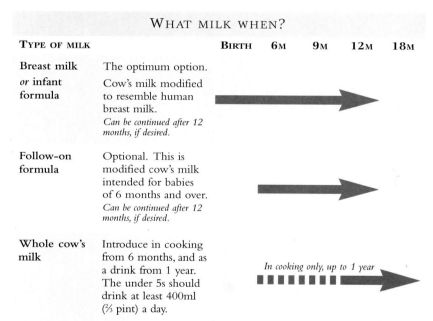

WHAT MILK WHEN?

TYPE OF MILK		BIRTH	6M	9M	12M	18M
Breast milk *or* **infant formula**	The optimum option. Cow's milk modified to resemble human breast milk. *Can be continued after 12 months, if desired.*					
Follow-on formula	Optional. This is modified cow's milk intended for babies of 6 months and over. *Can be continued after 12 months, if desired.*					
Whole cow's milk	Introduce in cooking from 6 months, and as a drink from 1 year. The under 5s should drink at least 400ml (⅔ pint) a day.			*In cooking only, up to 1 year*		

Water

Babies are vulnerable to dehydration and it is essential to maintain their fluid intake. If your baby is breast-fed, milk will supply the necessary fluids, but bottle-fed babies may need sips of water as formula is not so thirst-quenching. Once your baby is on a mainly solid diet, you will need to top up his fluid intake. Cooled boiled tap water is inexpensive, accessible and the best thirst-quencher. Young babies will need only a few sips of water, but it is wise to encourage your child to drink water from an early age: although there are many herbal and fruit drinks marketed for babies, most contain sugar, which can harm developing teeth and give your baby a taste for sweet drinks. Do not offer mineral water or use it to make up feeds: it is not bacteriologically safe unless boiled and may contain a higher level of sodium than is recommended for babies.

FAT

THE SOURCES OF SATURATED FAT: meat ◆ butter and margarine ◆ lard ◆ eggs ◆ cheese ◆ hydrogenated vegetable fat or oil, found in processed foods, such as biscuits.

THE SOURCES OF UNSATURATED FAT: olive oil ◆ sunflower oil ◆ corn oil ◆ sesame oil ◆ safflower oil ◆ oily fish.

FAT may be saturated or unsaturated. Saturated fat is derived mainly from animal sources and processed foods containing vegetable fat; unsaturated fat is derived from vegetable and fish sources. Saturated fats can increase blood cholesterol levels, and high intakes are linked to heart disease in adults. Whilst you should ensure that there is enough fat in your child's diet, it is a good idea to encourage healthy eating by choosing lean meat and using vegetable oils rather than butter for frying. Milk and cheese contain saturated fats but are also a good source of calcium, protein and vitamins. Children between the ages of 2 and 5 should get up to 35% of their total energy intake from fat. Up to the age of 1, children should derive 50% of their energy from fat.

PROTEIN

THE SOURCES OF PROTEIN: red meat ◆ poultry ◆ liver ◆ fish ◆ eggs ◆ milk ◆ cheese (but not cream cheese) ◆ grains ◆ pulses ◆ seeds.

PROTEIN is essential for growth and repair of body tissues; if we have an inadequate level of protein our resistance to disease and infection is lowered. Protein is made up of amino acids, some of which the body can manufacture, and some of which must be obtained from food. Animal proteins, including milk, contain all the amino acids the body needs, but soya is the only plant-based food that contains all these essential amino acids. Other foods must be combined in order to provide complete proteins: for example, grains can be combined with pulses or with a very small quantity of animal protein to provide a complete protein. Because protein is not stored by the body, foods containing protein should be eaten on most days. However, protein-rich foods should not be the major part of a baby's meal as a high-protein diet can put strain on immature kidneys. Protein deficiency is almost unheard of in the West.

CARBOHYDRATE

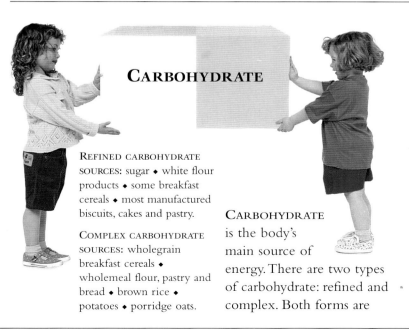

REFINED CARBOHYDRATE SOURCES: sugar ◆ white flour products ◆ some breakfast cereals ◆ most manufactured biscuits, cakes and pastry.

COMPLEX CARBOHYDRATE SOURCES: wholegrain breakfast cereals ◆ wholemeal flour, pastry and bread ◆ brown rice ◆ potatoes ◆ porridge oats.

CARBOHYDRATE is the body's main source of energy. There are two types of carbohydrate: refined and complex. Both forms are converted into blood sugar, thereby providing energy (calories). Refined carbohydrates, such as white bread and most sweet biscuits, are made up of ingredients that are stripped of their natural fibre during processing and have lost most of their valuable nutrients. Complex carbohydrates are energy-rich foods that retain their vitamins, minerals and fibre and are therefore more useful to the body. This form of carbohydrate should make up about 60% of your child's diet.

CALCIUM

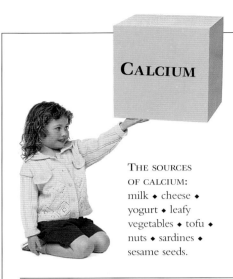

CALCIUM is important for the health and formation of bones and teeth. Two-thirds of a pint (400ml) of milk a day provides an adequate amount for children between the ages of 1 and 5.

THE SOURCES OF CALCIUM: milk ◆ cheese ◆ yogurt ◆ leafy vegetables ◆ tofu ◆ nuts ◆ sardines ◆ sesame seeds.

ZINC

ZINC is essential for normal growth and for the efficient function of the immune system. A varied diet should provide all the body's daily needs.

THE SOURCES OF ZINC: shellfish ◆ red meat ◆ peanuts ◆ sunflower seeds ◆ fortified breakfast cereals.

VITAMINS

VITAMINS are essential for the maintenance of a healthy body. Vitamins are either water-soluble (B complex and C) or fat-soluble (A, D, E and K). Water-soluble vitamins are destroyed by heat and, as their name indicates, dissolve in water, so foods rich in these vitamins should not be overcooked. Fat-soluble vitamins are stored in the body and may be harmful in large doses. Current guidelines recommend that all children under 5 take a supplement of vitamins A, C and D.

VITAMIN A (including beta-carotene and retinol) is essential for growth, fighting infection, healthy skin, good vision and strong bones. Good sources of retinol are: liver; eggs. Beta-carotene is an antioxidant that helps to protect against disease. Good sources are: carrots; red peppers; sweetcorn; tomatoes; sweet potatoes; melons; apricots; mangoes.

B COMPLEX VITAMINS, including folate, are needed for growth, a healthy nervous system and to aid digestion. Good sources are: meat, especially liver; tofu; sardines; eggs; nuts; dark green vegetables; dairy produce; wholegrain cereals; yeast extract; avocados; bananas.

VITAMIN C is required for growth, tissue repair, healthy skin, and to aid iron absorption. Good sources are: citrus fruits; strawberries; blackcurrants; kiwi fruit; dark green leafy vegetables; potatoes; peppers.

VITAMIN D is manufactured by skin exposed to sunlight, and is needed to absorb calcium and phosphorous for healthy bones and teeth. Good sources are: salmon; tuna; sardines; milk; cheese; eggs.

VITAMIN E is needed for the maintenance of the body's cell structure and it helps the body to create and maintain red blood cells. Good sources are: vegetable oils; wheatgerm; avocados; nuts.

IRON

THE SOURCES OF IRON: red meat, particularly liver ◆ oily fish ◆ pulses ◆ fortified baby rice ◆ fortified breakfast cereals ◆ bread ◆ green leafy vegetables ◆ dried fruit, especially dried apricots.

IRON is needed for both physical and mental development. Babies are born with a store of iron that lasts for about 6 months. After this time it is important to make sure they get the iron they need from their solids because iron deficiency, which can lead to anaemia if unchecked, leaves children feeling run-down and tired. A baby's iron requirements are particularly high between the ages of 6 and 12 months. Premature babies are especially vulnerable to iron depletion as their store of iron may last for only 6 weeks. If your baby was born prematurely, you may be advised by your doctor to give him an iron supplement until he is 1 year old. (See page 53 for further information.)

FOOD ALLERGIES & INTOLERANCE

WHAT IS A FOOD ALLERGY?

An allergic reaction occurs when the immune system perceives a harmless substance as a threat and overreacts, triggering unpleasant, occasionally dangerous, side-effects. Because young babies' immune systems are not fully developed, they are more likely to become sensitized to common allergens, such as eggs and gluten, which is why the introduction of these foods should be delayed. Children who do experience a food allergy may well outgrow it by the age of 3, but occasionally an allergy will persist and the only option is avoidance.

A FAMILY HISTORY OF ALLERGIES

If your family has a history of food allergy or atopic disease (e.g. hay fever, asthma, urticaria or eczema) it is recommended that your baby is exclusively breast-fed for the first 4–6 months, and that foods likely to cause allergy are not introduced before 6 months at the earliest. Begin weaning with low-allergen foods, such as rice, potato, pear and apple, and introduce foods one at a time so that any adverse reactions can be traced to the "trigger" food. It can be difficult to pinpoint which, if any, foods provoke an allergic response and it should be remembered that other factors besides food (such as house dust, pets or bath products) can trigger these reactions. If there is a history of allergy to a particular food, avoid that food until your child is at least 1 year old. However, do not remove key foods from your child's diet without first consulting a doctor. If you suspect that your child is allergic to a common food, such as milk or wheat, you should seek expert advice on planning a balanced diet.

COW'S MILK (PROTEIN) ALLERGY

An allergic reaction to one of the proteins found in cow's milk, cow's milk-based infant formulas and dairy products can give rise to diverse symptoms, namely diarrhoea, vomiting, abdominal pains, eczema and lactose intolerance (see below). Babies who experience this allergic reaction can be given a soya-based or hypoallergenic formula milk, on the advice of a doctor, if breast milk is not an option. Older children need a dairy-free diet (consult a doctor or dietitian).

NUT ALLERGY

Although allergy to tree nuts is relatively rare, the peanut is the trigger for one of the most severe allergic reactions, anaphylactic shock (in which the throat swells and breathing becomes difficult). In families with a history of any kind of food allergy, it is advisable to avoid all products containing peanuts or unrefined peanut oil until the child is 3 years old. If there is no history of allergy, peanuts of a suitable consistency (e.g. smooth peanut butter) can be introduced from 6 months.

LACTOSE INTOLERANCE

Lactose is the sugar in milk and lactose intolerance is the inability to digest this sugar because of a lack of a digestive enzyme, called lactase, in the gut. The condition, whose main symptom is diarrhoea, is usually caused by gastroenteritis bacteria or viruses damaging the gut where lactase is produced. Once the gut has recovered and repaired the damage (which may take anything from a few days to a few weeks), the enzyme will be produced once more and the intolerance will disappear. While the condition lasts, it can be managed by using either a soya-based formula (available only on prescription) or a low-lactose infant formula.

GLUTEN INTOLERANCE

Wheat, barley, oats, and their products, contain gluten and this substance can provoke similar symptoms to lactose intolerance. Gluten intolerance may co-exist with lactose intolerance and result from gut damage after an attack of gastroenteritis. Foods containing gluten should not be introduced into any baby's diet before 6 months. Gluten-free cereals, such as rice, millet and maize, can be introduced from 4 months. If there is a family history of gluten intolerance, your baby should follow a gluten-free diet for at least the first year. In most cases, the condition disappears once the gut has had time to recover from the gastroenteritic illness. Chronic gluten intolerance is coeliac disease. This condition requires proper dietary management if diagnosed. It is thought that the availability of the more highly modified whey-based formula milks and the later introduction of solid foods has led to a dramatic drop in the incidence of coeliac disease.

Store Cupboard

A WELL-STOCKED STORE CUPBOARD is invaluable in any kitchen. It should work as a fail-safe so that if you haven't had time to go shopping, you can use ingredients already to hand in your kitchen to make a quick and nutritious meal for your children, or indeed for the whole family. While the lists of foods on these pages are by no means exhaustive, they represent a useful and highly versatile selection of stand-by foods.

Dried staple foods

Bread and other grain products, such as pasta and rice, are invaluable carbohydrate sources that can be used as the basis for many quick, healthy meals. Although dried beans and pulses generally require some advance preparation, they are both nutritious and economical. In addition to the items listed right, stock: Plain flour • self-raising flour • wholemeal flour • cornflour • Chinese egg noodles • taco shells.

BREAD PRODUCTS, such as wholemeal and white bread; bread sticks; muffins.

BEANS AND PULSES, for example, red kidney beans; red and green lentils; haricot beans.

RICE, particularly baby rice for purées; white and brown long-grain rice; risotto rice.

PASTA, including soup pasta; farfalle and fusilli; spaghetti; lasagne sheets; cannelloni tubes.

COUSCOUS and other wheat products, such as semolina and bulgar wheat.

DRIED FRUIT, including apricots; mangoes; peaches; prunes; apple rings; raisins.

Breakfast cereals

Choose low-sugar cereals made with rice, oats or wheat. A wholegrain variety is preferable, but avoid bran-based products with added fibre. Alternatively, make a mixed-grain muesli. Use fresh or dried fruits, rather than refined sugar, to sweeten cereals.

COMMERCIAL CEREALS, for instance, corn flakes; puffed rice; wheat biscuits; malted mini wheat biscuits.

MUESLI, made with a mixture of rolled oats, mixed grains, toasted wheatgerm and chopped dried fruit.

HIDDEN SUGARS

◆ BREAKFAST CEREALS may contain more than 45% sugar in different forms, e.g. maltose, honey, glucose and dextrose, and these may be listed separately, making it harder to judge the total content.

Dairy products

Choose full-fat, pasteurized milk and dairy products for children under 5 years old.

EGGS

Eggs make a nutritious meal in minutes. Choose free-range eggs and store in a refrigerator.

CHEESES, such as soft cream cheese for dips and spreads; mild or medium Cheddar; Edam or Gruyère; cottage cheese; fresh Parmesan.

MILK should be full-fat and pasteurized, whether cow's or goat's milk. Keep a pint of long-life milk in the cupboard as a standby.

YOGURT, particularly full-fat natural yogurt; low-sugar fruit or vanilla yogurts (preferably a live, organic variety); fromage frais.

BUTTER (an unsalted or lightly salted variety) or a good quality margarine for spreading on bread or for shallow frying and baking.

Sauces, oils & seasonings

A plentiful supply of bottled sauces and oils, herbs and spices will give plenty of culinary scope.

SAUCES & FLAVOURINGS, such as soy sauce; oyster sauce; tomato purée; Worcestershire sauce; pesto; vegetable and chicken stock-cubes.

OILS & VINEGARS for cooking and salad dressings, including olive oil; sunflower oil; vegetable oil; sesame oil; balsamic and wine vinegars.

HERBS, for example, mixed dried herbs; bay leaves; oregano; thyme; prepared bouquets garnis; fresh basil; fresh and dried parsley.

SPICES, such as powdered cinnamon, mixed spice and ginger for baking; nutmeg (buy the whole spice); fresh root ginger; mild paprika.

Frozen foods

Many vegetables and fruits, such as peas and sweetcorn, are frozen within 2–3 hours of being picked, ensuring that they retain valuable nutrients. In fact, fresh vegetables that are stored for several days often contain fewer nutrients than frozen vegetables.

Frozen chicken portions and fish fillets are good standbys. If buying fish pieces in breadcrumbs, choose larger portion sizes as there will be less coating in proportion to fish. Freeze bread and butter for emergencies, and good dairy ice-cream for quick puddings.

Canned foods

Some canned processed foods are high in sugar, salt and saturated fat, so always read labels carefully. However, many canned products are valuable nutritionally. Stock: canned tuna • sardines • baked beans • kidney beans • plum tomatoes • sweetcorn.

ADDITIVES

◆ CHECK INGREDIENTS lists as some common commercial additives, such as the food colourings annato and tartrazine, have been known to provoke allergic reactions in young children.

Equipment

YOU WILL PROBABLY find that you already have most of the equipment needed to make home-cooked meals for your child, but certain items will facilitate food preparation and prove useful for general family cooking. Feeding equipment need not be expensive or complicated, but you should look for items that will make preparing solids easy for you and that will later help your baby to learn how to feed himself.

Processors & blenders

Electric food processors, liquidizers or hand blenders make it easy to purée large quantities of food quickly. Some foods, such as cooked apples, will purée to a smooth consistency in a blender or processor; other foods should be strained after puréeing.

MINI PROCESSORS are useful for making baby foods in small portions.

MINI BOWL

HAND-HELD BLENDERS are easy to clean, and ideal for puréeing small quantities in the container provided with the blender.

FULL-SIZE PROCESSORS facilitate cooking in large batches, but a mini bowl attachment will work better for small quantities.

MOULIS purée foods while holding back any indigestible husks or skins.

A METAL-MESH SIEVE can be used to eliminate any fibrous material from purées for babies.

Freezer containers

Tiny portions of purée for babies can be frozen in ice-cube trays (see page 18). You can also buy small pots that hold larger portions of food. These can be transferred straight from the freezer to the microwave. Mini freezer boxes and yogurt pots are also useful.

ICE-CUBE TRAY made of flexible plastic allows you to freeze meal-size portions.

FREEZER POTS with snap-on lids are useful for storing and are easily transportable.

Steamers

A multi-layered steamer allows you to cook several foods simultaneously. A collapsible steamer that fits various sizes of pan is a versatile alternative.

STACKED STEAMER

COLLAPSIBLE STEAMER

Baby chairs

A bouncy chair that supports the back is ideal for the early stages of feeding. At around 6 months, your baby will probably then progress to a rigid highchair with safety harness. A clip-on chair with a safety harness is a lightweight, transportable, space-saving alternative.

CLIP-ON CHAIRS may be clamped to a sturdy table that can take the extra weight. Do not clamp them over a cloth.

HIGHCHAIRS should be wide-based and sturdy, with a wipe-clean tray.

BOUNCY CHAIRS are lightweight seats that are ideal for babies who cannot yet sit unaided.

Feeding kit

There are many varieties of feeding bowls and spoons available. All that is needed to start with is a small weaning bowl and a shallow plastic weaning spoon, preferably one made of soft, flexible plastic that will not hurt tender gums. Later on, bowls with suction pads, or with thermal linings, feeding cups and special children's cutlery become useful.

WEANING BOWLS should be made of heat-proof plastic. Choose one with a hand-grip.

HEAT-SENSITIVE BOWLS and spoons change colour to indicate if food is too hot.

SUCTION-PADS on bowls allow them to be secured to highchair trays.

WEANING SPOON

TEAT

Cap for straw

GRADUATED FEEDING CUP

Rigid spout

WEANING SPOONS should have a small shallow bowl with no hard edges.

SOFT SPOUT

FEEDING CUP

FEEDING CUPS enable babies to take fluids independently. Most babies graduate from bottles to cups with a spout and snap-tight lid to an open cup. Non-spill multi-way beakers are ideal.

Bibs

Feeding can be a messy business, for young babies, parents, and even the surrounding wallpaper. Protect your baby's clothes from the worst of the mess with bibs, and use a large square plastic splash mat, or just an old plastic tablecloth, under feeding chairs.

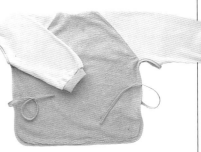

SOFT COTTON BIBS should have a plastic backing and a velcro fastener.

PELICAN BIBS with a shallow trough are suitable for older babies.

BIBS WITH SLEEVES and ties at the back give the best protection.

Preparing Baby Food

YOU DON'T NEED any special expertise to prepare baby foods, but there are ways to streamline the process so that even busy parents can make foods that perfectly suit their baby's needs. Many first foods, such as mashed banana and avocado, make excellent baby purées and do not require any cooking. For other meals, you can either set aside unseasoned portions of food, such as vegetables, that are being cooked for the rest of the family, or cook batches of puréed foods specifically for your baby. The cooking methods shown on these two pages are useful for making the smooth purées suitable for the early stages of weaning (see pages 28–31 for recipes).

DIFFERENT COOKING TECHNIQUES

◆ STEAMING helps to preserve the taste and nutrient content of fresh produce. The water-soluble vitamins B and C can be destroyed by overcooking: broccoli loses 60% of its vitamin C if boiled, 20% if steamed.

◆ BOILING can destroy nutrients so ingredients should be cooked just until tender in the minimum amount of water. Be careful not to overcook.

◆ MICROWAVING allows fast cooking of fruits and vegetables (and later fish) with minimal nutrient loss. When fresh ingredients are cooked rapidly at full power, most of the nutrients are retained.

◆ BAKING is a nutrient-retaining, labour-saving cooking method. Potatoes, sweet potatoes and squashes can be washed, pricked with a fork and baked until tender. The flesh can then be scooped out and mashed.

Blending purées

2 Engage the food processor motor until a smooth, even-textured purée is produced. If necessary, add a little of the cooking water to thin the mixture, then pulse briefly.

1 Cook small pieces of vegetable or fruit until tender. Drain, retaining a tablespoon or two of the cooking liquid, then pour into the food processor bowl.

3 The final texture of the purée should be completely smooth. It can be thinned with cooled boiled water for young babies.

Making purées with a mouli

1 To make a purée from fibrous ingredients, e.g. garden peas, fit the fine mouli blade then place the ingredients in the mouli and set over a bowl.

Rotate the handle to push the pulp through the blades

Ingredients should be chopped into fairly uniform pieces

2 Turn the mouli handle to rotate the blade. Continue the grinding until most of the ingredients are pushed through the mouli, then discard the fibrous pulp left behind.

The mouli produces a smooth, thick, pulpy mixture

3 The finished purée has a smooth, uniform texture. It can be thinned down with a little of the water reserved from cooking, if necessary.

ORGANIC PRODUCE & PREPARING BABY FOODS

Growing demand has led to a greater variety of organic foods on the market. The use of pesticides and fertilisers is controlled by law, but there is as yet no firm evidence to show that foods grown without pesticides or artificial fertilisers are healthier. Organic farming is an environmentally friendly option, but it generates higher prices, and parents should not feel that a non-organic diet is unhealthy. However, precautions can be taken: any residues in fresh produce are most likely to be in the skin, so remove any peel and discard the outer leaves of cabbages, lettuces, etc. If pesticides have been *absorbed* into the food, these measures will make no difference, but there is no evidence of any child being harmed by eating non-organic produce.

Freezing & Reheating

BATCH-COOKING AND FREEZING is by far the most time-economical way to make food for your baby. Only a few purées – banana, avocado, melon and aubergine, for example – do not freeze well. Food should be stored in a freezer that freezes food to 0°F (-18°C) or below in 24 hours. Food that has thawed should never be refrozen, though defrosted raw food may be cooked and then frozen again for later use.

Using frozen purées

1 Allow the freshly cooked purée to cool to room temperature then spoon it into sterilized ice-cube trays. Transfer the trays to the freezer.

2 When the purée has frozen solid, take the trays from the freezer and quickly push out the cubes on to a clean plate.

3 Set aside the required number of cubes and heat in a pan or microwave until piping hot all the way through (see below).

4 Transfer the remaining purée portions to a freezer bag, seal tightly, then label and date the contents. Return to the freezer.

Reheating rules

It is safe to thaw purées in a microwave or saucepan, as long as the food is then heated all the way through until piping hot. If using a microwave, be particularly vigilant as microwaves can heat food unevenly, producing "hot spots" but leaving other parts of the food cold. Let the purée cool after heating, and test the temperature before offering it to your baby. It is dangerous to reheat food more than once so reheat only one portion at a time to avoid unnecessary waste.

FREEZER STORAGE TIMES	
TYPE	TIMING
Breast milk	1 month
Vegetable purées	6 months
Fruit purées	6 months
Purées with milk	2 months
Cooked fish dishes	3 months
Cooked meat dishes	3 months
Bread	2 months
Butter	6 months
Vegetables	6 months
Raw fish	3 months
Raw sausages/mince	1 month
Other raw meat	3 months

Food Hygiene

BABIES AND YOUNG CHILDREN are especially vulnerable to the effects of food poisoning, so it is essential that great care is taken in the storage and preparation of their food. In the first few months of a baby's life, extra care must be taken (see below), but once your baby is mobile and exploring objects with his mouth, there is little point in sterilizing anything except bottles and teats. Attention to food safety rules, however, remains crucial.

Sterilizing equipment

Warm milk is the perfect breeding ground for bacteria, so bottles must be scrupulously washed and sterilized. Sterilize all bottles, teats and feeding cup spouts up to 1 year, and sterilize feeding spoons for the first 6 months. You can use an electric, steam or microwave sterilizing kit, or simply boil feeding equipment in a pan of water for 10 minutes, or wash it in a dishwasher on a hot programme.

MICROWAVE STEAM STERILIZER

STERILIZING BY BOILING

General hygiene

Kitchen hygiene need not be complicated; adhering to a few simple rules will minimize the likelihood of food contamination: you should always wash your hands before preparing food, and your child's hands should be washed before eating. It is also a good idea to wipe daily with an anti-bacterial agent any surfaces that come into contact with your baby's food. Chopping boards and kitchen knives should be washed immediately after use, and equipment left to air-dry, and only perfectly clean tea towels should be used to dry your baby's feeding equipment.

FOOD SAFETY TIPS

◆ KEEP RAW MEAT, FISH AND EGGS away from other foods. Wash hands thoroughly after contact with any of these foods and use separate chopping boards for meat and fish and raw fruit and vegetables.

◆ ONLY REHEAT FOOD ONCE, and make sure it is reheated to a high temperature to kill off the bacteria.

◆ DO NOT KEEP your baby's half-eaten food for a later meal because the saliva introduced from your baby's spoon will breed bacteria quickly.

◆ ALWAYS DATE FOOD stored in the freezer so that food which is past its best, or which has even deteriorated and become harmful, is never offered.

◆ DO NOT LEAVE FOOD unrefrigerated as bacteria multiply rapidly at room temperature, and cool food quickly if it is to be refrigerated or frozen.

◆ COVER ALL FOOD AND DRINK securely to protect it from contamination by germ-carrying insects, and keep pets away from food and kitchen work surfaces.

4-6
Months

FOR YOUR YOUNG BABY, THE FIRST TASTE OF
SOLIDS AND THE BEGINNING OF WEANING
IS A SIGNIFICANT POINT IN HER DEVELOPMENT.
YOU MAY FIND THAT YOUR BABY TAKES TO NEW
TASTES AND TEXTURES IMMEDIATELY, OR YOU MAY
ENCOUNTER A LITTLE INITIAL WARINESS, BUT IF
YOU ATTUNE YOURSELF TO YOUR BABY'S INDIVIDUAL
NEEDS, THIS SHOULD BE AN ENJOYABLE TIME OF
LEARNING AND EXPLORATION FOR YOU BOTH.

Starting solids

THE FIRST YEAR of life is a period of rapid growth and development, with most babies at least doubling their birthweight by the time they reach 6 months. For the first 6 months or so, breast milk or formula provides all the nutrients your baby needs, and indeed should remain the main source of nourishment. However, at around 4 months she will reach a stage when she needs more concentrated sources of calories. Her first taste of solid food will be a significant milestone and mark the beginning of a gradual shift to a solid diet.

When does my baby need solids?

Don't be in a hurry to wean your baby on to solids because milk provides all the nutrients she needs in the first 6 months or so. Current medical advice is that solids should be withheld until at least 16 weeks after a baby's due date. A very young baby's digestive and immune systems are not sufficiently developed before this time and there is a higher risk of food allergy occurring (see page 11). Accordingly, if your baby was born prematurely, you may need to wait longer before beginning weaning. While sucking is a natural reflex, so too is gagging on unaccustomed solids. Babies have to be ready to learn the new skill of pushing food to the back of the mouth with their tongues and swallowing.

RECOGNIZING THE SIGNS

At around 16–20 weeks, your baby may show signs of being ready for her first taste of solids. She may no longer seem satisfied by her usual milk feeds and may become increasingly unsettled. If she has been sleeping through the night, she may start waking again to demand a feed. She might start showing interest in the things you eat, too.

TAKING THE LEAD FROM YOUR BABY
Do not rush to introduce solids at the minimum recommended age. Look for signs from your baby that he is ready to try solids.

Foods for weaning

CHOOSING STARTER FOODS

Plain baby rice, mixed with expressed breast milk or formula, is a good starter food, but you can also introduce single-ingredient purées during the first 4 weeks of weaning. Simple purées enable you to assess how each new food has suited your child, and accustom her to a wide range of single fruits and vegetables before they are mixed together. Avoid any foods that might cause early allergies (see page 11). Root vegetables tend to be the most popular with young babies because of their naturally sweet flavour and smooth texture once puréed. Dessert apples and pears are ideal first fruits but taste them yourself before cooking as they must be ripe and naturally sweet.

Remember that baby rice is an excellent mixer too, as it can make strong-flavoured foods more palatable to some babies. Alternatively, foods such as mashed banana, papaya or avocado make nutritionally excellent no-cook purées.

WHY HOMEMADE IS BEST

If you make baby food yourself, you can be sure of using only the best ingredients, without the need for thickeners or additives. It is also more economical, and easier to establish a varied diet with food combinations designed to suit your baby. Homemade food has a fresher taste than commercial baby food, which may contain preservatives. Bought baby purées tend to be uniform and bland.

Getting started

Preparing tiny amounts of purée is time-consuming, so batch-cook and freeze portions, perhaps once a week (see page 18). Remember that at first your baby will only manage a "solid" consistency similar to runny yogurt, so the thickness of your prepared purées will change over the weeks. Alternatively, your baby's food can be prepared alongside the rest of the family's: if you are cooking vegetables for your supper, for example, simply cook without adding any seasoning, set aside a small portion for your baby and purée it in a blender when she is ready for her meal.

SPECIAL EQUIPMENT

You will find suggestions for food preparation equipment on page 14. Your baby can take her first taste of solids from the tip of your finger, but once she is more accustomed to solids, you can use a small plastic weaning spoon and bowl. Plastic spoons have rounded edges that are kinder to tender gums. The spoon should be shallow too, so that your baby can easily suck the food from it. The bowl may have a handle that allows you to hold it up to your baby. Cover her clothes with a bib and have some wipes, or a damp cloth, on hand.

IDEAL FOODS

◆ DESSERT APPLE ◆ PEAR ◆ PAPAYA ◆ BANANA ◆ AVOCADO ◆ BROCCOLI ◆ CARROT ◆ POTATO ◆ SWEET POTATO ◆ SQUASH OR PUMPKIN (SEE PAGES 26-7).

REMEMBER

◆ ALWAYS WASH YOUR hands thoroughly before preparing or offering food, and wash your baby's hands before feeds.

◆ FOR THINNING PURÉES to the desired consistency of runny yogurt, use cooled boiled tap water, a little cooking water, or your baby's usual milk.

◆ DO NOT USE bottled mineral waters in feeds as they are not sterile and also tend to have a high sodium content.

◆ FEEDING BOTTLES and spoons should be sterilized for the first 12 months, and bowls should be immersed in boiling water for 10 minutes or washed in a dishwasher (see page 19). Use a clean tea towel to dry utensils.

WEANING BOWL AND SPOON

Begin with 1 tablespoon of purée that is the consistency of runny yogurt.

Introducing your baby to solids

Pick a time of day for your baby's feed when you are not rushed or likely to be distracted. If possible, choose the same time every day (perhaps lunchtime) so that you can begin to establish a routine. You may want to give your baby half her usual milk feed before her solids so that she is not frantically hungry.

TESTING THE TEMPERATURE
Food should be room temperature or lukewarm. If using a microwave, heat the food until piping hot throughout, allow to cool then stir well and check the temperature before feeding it to your baby.

JUDGING QUANTITIES
All babies' appetites and needs are different, but you will probably find that your baby initially takes 1–2 teaspoons of purée, so allow 1 tablespoon (15ml) or 1 ice-cube portion. As she develops, offer a little more and continue the feed until her interest starts to wane. When she has had enough of the solids, finish off with the second half of her milk feed.

TAKING IT SLOWLY
Even though your baby may relish her solid food from the start, it will still take time for her to master the art of swallowing it. Let her enjoy her mealtimes, by being relaxed yourself and taking things at your baby's pace. Avoid times when she is over-tired or restless. Talk to her encouragingly and make sure she is comfortable, whether she is in a bouncy seat, or cuddled on your lap. Show her that the experience is enjoyable by smiling and making eye contact and be prepared to get a little bit smeared with baby rice too.

THE FIRST FEEDING EXPERIENCE
Your baby will probably feel calm and reassured if you choose a quiet time to begin her feed. Cradle her on your lap, supporting her upper body and head to make swallowing easy.

FIRST TASTES

Wash your hands thoroughly then dip the tip of your finger into the food to test its temperature. If it is cool enough, let your baby suck the food from your finger to accustom her to the taste. The feel of your finger is probably familiar to her and lessens the strangeness of tasting "solids." You can then introduce a spoon. Have two to hand in case you drop one.

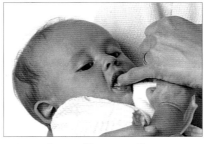

1 At first, offer a small amount of purée from the tip of your scrupulously clean finger and let her suck the food.

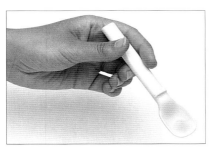

2 Coat the tip of a soft shallow weaning spoon with purée; don't overload it as this will make your baby splutter.

3 Place the spoon just between her lips, and let her suck the food off. If she spits the purée out, scrape it up and offer it again.

If your baby rejects food

Your baby may be one of the many who refuse solids at the first try. Be patient, it doesn't mean that she will never eat them. Wait and try again the next day. Initially, you are offering solids purely to introduce your baby to different foods. It is vital not to cut down on the amount of milk you give as at this point solids are not replacing any part of her milk diet. If your baby seems to dislike a certain purée, try mixing it with a familiar or bland taste, such as breast milk, baby rice or puréed potato, to make a gentler introduction. If this does not work, simply stop offering that food and try it again at a later date. Weaning is unlikely to take an uninterrupted course; there may be days when your baby refuses solids, perhaps if she is feeling unwell or is in an unfamiliar environment, and wants only her comforting milk feed. Don't be anxious about this: a short break from solids will not harm your baby. Try reintroducing solid food after a few days, or prepare a runnier purée that is easier for your baby to swallow. At this early stage, as long as your baby is getting her nutrition from milk, and as long as she continues to gain weight over a period of several days, she is probably getting enough food.

TAKING IT GENTLY
Follow your baby's lead during feeding. She may take a little time to become accustomed to solids, but increased familiarity will bring reassurance.

First Foods

VERY FIRST FOODS must be easy to digest and made of ingredients that will gently accustom your baby to new flavours and textures. You may find that your baby immediately likes quite strong flavours, such as sweet potato, parsnip or carrot, but some babies seem to prefer to begin with the more familiar tastes of milky baby rice or a bland potato purée. To begin with, purées should be quite runny and absolutely smooth, similar in consistency to runny yogurt, and made up of only one or two ingredients.

BABY RICE
Specially formulated baby rice has a fine texture and is often fortified with minerals and iron, and can be mixed with cooled boiled tap water, breast or formula milk. It is easily digested and its milky taste makes an easy transition to solids. Choose a sugar-free variety, and make it according to packet instructions.

POTATO PURÉE
The mild taste of potato makes it a good weaning food for young babies. Use only floury textured potatoes and make the purée by pressing mashed potato through a sieve. Do not use a food processor: it breaks down the starches and produces a sticky pulp. (See First Vegetable Purée on page 28.)

CARROT PURÉE
Carrots, like many other root vegetables, blend well and have a naturally sweet taste that tends to appeal to babies. They should be steamed or boiled and blended with a spoonful of cooking water or your baby's usual milk to create a smooth-textured purée. (See First Vegetable Purée on page 28.)

BROCCOLI & POTATO PURÉE
Broccoli is a good source of essential vitamins and can be blended to a smooth purée after brief steaming. However, babies may find its strong flavour distasteful so it is best combined with sieved boiled potato (see left) or baby rice to make a creamy purée. (See page 30 for recipe.)

SOME IDEAL FOODS

  YOUNG COURGETTES make a smooth purée that can be sieved for very young babies. Large courgettes may be unpleasantly bitter.

  BUTTERNUT SQUASH is a good source of vitamin A. Although it can be steamed, its sweetness is enhanced by baking.

CANTALOUPE MELON is the best source of vitamins A and C, but Galia tends to be sweeter than other melon varieties.

 PARSNIP has a distinctly sweet taste that babies enjoy. It should be sieved after puréeing to remove any traces of fibre.

 ORANGE-FLESHED SWEET POTATO is an excellent source of beta-carotene and makes a sweet, soft, smooth purée.

 PAPAYA needs no cooking if fully ripe. It can be puréed or mashed on its own or with a little formula or breast milk.

PEAR PURÉE

Sweet ripe pear cooked in a little water until soft then blended makes an appealing first fruit purée for babies. Once your baby is 5 months old, there is no need to cook pears before puréeing, provided the fruit you choose is perfectly ripe and juicy. (See First Fruit Purée on page 29.)

APPLE PURÉE

Sweet eating apple varieties make a smooth apple sauce. Once your baby has become accustomed to the taste, this purée can be mixed with other fruits. Try combining apple purée with a little baby rice or specially formulated baby yogurt for a creamier finish. (See First Fruit Purée on page 29.)

BANANA PURÉE

A fully ripe banana makes an instant purée when thoroughly mashed. Its naturally sticky consistency can be modified by adding a little expressed breast milk or formula. Heating a banana in a microwave for a few seconds will make it easier to mash. (See First Fruit Purée on page 29.)

BABY RICE & DRIED APRICOT

Dried apricots are rich in beta-carotene and iron and useful when ripe summer fruits are scarce. Simmer soft, ready-to-eat apricots and press through a sieve to remove the skins. For a gentle introduction to this fruit, purée with baby rice. (See Dried Apricot Purée on page 31.)

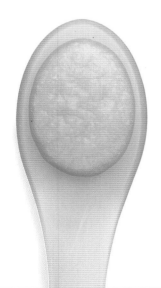   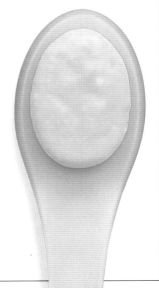

FIRST VEGETABLE PURÉE

250g (8oz) carrots or floury potatoes (or a mixture of the two), peeled

Your baby's first foods should be mild in taste, easy to digest, completely smooth and unlikely to provoke an allergic reaction. Begin with single-ingredient purées in the first week or two, and then progress to combinations of root vegetables (see pages 22–25 for advice).

1 Chop the carrots or potatoes into small pieces. Put in a steamer or colander set over boiling water and cook for about 15 minutes, or until tender. Alternatively, place in a pan, pour over just enough boiling water to cover and simmer, covered, for 15 minutes, or until soft.

2 Blend the vegetable to a purée using some of the liquid from the bottom of the steamer or the pan (see page 16).

3 Spoon a little purée into your baby's bowl and serve lukewarm. Pour the remainder into sterilized ice-cube trays and freeze (see page 18).

VARIATION

Substitute other root vegetables, such as parsnip or swede. Chop, cook and blend as described above.

 Preparation/cooking
5 minutes/15 minutes

 Makes 8 portions

 Suitable for freezing

See page 26 for illustrations.

——— TIPS ———
The amount of liquid needed depends on whether your baby finds swallowing difficult. A general rule is to make an absolutely smooth, very runny purée, akin to runny yogurt.

Do not purée potato or sweet potato in a food processor as the mixture will become starchy and gluey. Use a mouli or sieve to purée potato.

CREAMY VEGETABLE PURÉE

1 tbsp sugar-free, vitamin- and iron-enriched baby rice

3 tbsp formula or breast milk

4 tbsp first vegetable purée (see above)

Strong-tasting root vegetable purées, such as parsnip or carrot, may be made milder with the addition of baby rice. Baby rice also combines well with steamed and puréed broccoli and cauliflower.

1 Mix together the baby rice and milk, according to package instructions, and stir into the vegetable purée until thoroughly combined.

2 Spoon a little purée into your baby's bowl and serve lukewarm. Pour the remainder into sterilized ice-cube trays and freeze (see page 18).

 Preparation/cooking
5 minutes/2 minutes

 Makes 6 portions

 Suitable for freezing

FIRST FRUIT PURÉE

2 medium dessert apples or ripe pears, peeled and cored

1–2 tbsp water

Choose only sweet, completely ripe fruit for your baby. This will be a little thinner than a vegetable purée. Apple and pear purée mix together well.

1 Chop your chosen fruit into small, even-sized pieces. Put the pieces into a heavy-based saucepan with the water, cover and cook over a low heat until tender (about 10 minutes for apples, 4 minutes for pears).

2 Blend the fruit to a smooth purée using some of the cooking liquid, adding more cooled boiled water to thin it, if desired (see page 16).

3 Spoon a little purée into your baby's bowl and serve lukewarm. Pour the remainder into sterilized ice-cube trays and freeze (see page 18).

VARIATION

Mash a raw banana or half a papaya and purée with approximately 2 tablespoons of breast or formula milk. If necessary, the banana can be heated in a microwave for a few seconds to make it easier to mash. These purées are not suitable for freezing.

 Preparation/cooking
5 minutes/5–10 minutes

 Makes 6 portions

 Suitable for freezing

See page 27 for illustrations.

— TIP —

All fruits for very first purées, except for banana, papaya and avocado, must be cooked. At 5 months you can use raw peach, mango, plum and melon, if they are ripe and juicy.

FRUITY BABY RICE

1 tbsp sugar-free, vitamin- and iron-enriched baby rice

3 tbsp formula or breast milk

4 tbsp first fruit purée (see above)

Baby rice is a valuable first food: it is easily digested and has a milky taste that helps to ease your baby's transition from a purely milk diet to solids. It may be served plain or combined with a purée.

1 Mix together the baby rice and milk, according to package instructions, and stir into the fruit purée to give it a slightly creamy texture.

2 Spoon a little purée into your baby's bowl and serve lukewarm. Pour the remainder into sterilized ice-cube trays and freeze (see page 18).

 Preparation/cooking
5 minutes/2 minutes

 Makes 6 portions

 Suitable for freezing

SIMPLE VEGETABLE PURÉES

*Denotes recipes that are not suitable for freezing.

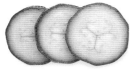

COURGETTE

COURGETTE

Courgette can be used alone or mixed with carrot or potato purée (see First Vegetable Purée, page 28). Makes 8 servings.

Trim and slice 250g (8oz) courgettes. Place in a steamer and cook until tender, about 12 minutes. Alternatively, put in a pan with water to cover, bring to the boil and simmer for 6 minutes. Blend to a purée then strain, if desired.

POTATO

BUTTERNUT SQUASH OR PUMPKIN

Squashes are a good source of beta-carotene. Butternut squash combines well with puréed apple, pear or peach (see First Fruit Purée, page 29). Makes 8 servings.

Peel and deseed a 500g (1lb) squash or slice of pumpkin then cut into small pieces. Cook as described for First Vegetable Purée on page 28, then blend to a purée, adding a little cooking water if necessary. Alternatively, cut the squash in half, scoop out the seeds and brush with melted butter. Cover with foil and bake in an oven preheated to 180°C/ 350°F/gas 4 for 1½ hours, or until tender.

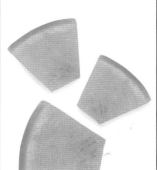

BUTTERNUT SQUASH

SWEET POTATO

The orange-fleshed sweet potato is an excellent source of beta-carotene. It blends well with apple, pear or peach purée (see First Fruit Purée, page 29). Makes 8 servings.

Scrub 300g (10oz) sweet potatoes, pat dry and prick with a fork. Bake in an oven preheated to 200°C/400°F/gas 6 for 45 minutes–1 hour. Scoop out the flesh and mash together with 1–2 tablespoons of formula or breast milk. Alternatively, peel and cube the sweet potatoes and cook as described for First Vegetable Purée on page 28.

SWEET POTATO

CAULIFLOWER OR BROCCOLI

Cauliflower and broccoli have strong tastes and are best mixed with potato purée (see First Vegetable Purée, page 28) or baby rice. Makes 6 servings.

Place 250g (8oz) of small cauliflower or broccoli florets in a steamer and cook until tender, about 10 minutes. Drain and blend to a purée.

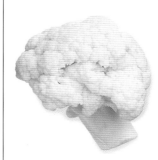

CAULIFLOWER

BROCCOLI

SIMPLE FRUIT PURÉES

MELON*

Melon makes a refreshing purée and combines well with mashed banana or avocado. Galia melons tend to be the sweetest variety. Makes 1 serving.

Take a small wedge of melon, remove the seeds and cut the flesh away from the skin, discarding the greener flesh near the skin. Blend to a purée of the desired consistency.

GALIA MELON

HONEYDEW MELON

PEACH OR NECTARINE*

Fresh, ripe peaches can be puréed on their own or mixed with baby rice, banana or pear (see First Fruit Purée, page 29). They are suitable for babies over 5 months old. Makes 2 servings.

Score a cross on the base of a ripe peach or nectarine, then submerge in boiling water for 1 minute. Skin and chop the peach flesh, then purée in a blender. (Ripe, sweet peaches, nectarines, plums and mangoes can be used raw.)

DRIED APRICOT

Dried, ready-to-eat apricots are rich in nutrients and useful when seasonal fruits are scarce. This is good mixed with baby rice or apple or pear purée (see First Fruit Purée, page 29). Makes 4 servings.

Simmer a handful of apricots in a little water for about 10 minutes, or until tender. Purée in a blender to the desired consistency using as much of the cooking liquid as is needed to make a smooth pulp. Work the pulp through a mouli or strong-meshed sieve to remove the fibrous skins.

NECTARINE

DRIED APRICOTS

AVOCADO*

Avocado is very nutritious and has a buttery flavour and texture that is generally popular with babies. It combines well with papaya, pear or banana. Choose a soft, ripe fruit and prepare just before your baby is ready to eat (to avoid discoloration). Makes 1 serving.

Halve the avocado, scoop out the stone and mash half the flesh with a fork, or purée to the desired consistency with about 2 tablespoons of breast or formula milk.

AVOCADO

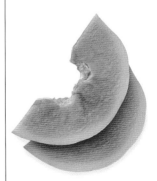

PAPAYA

6-9
Months

ONCE YOUR BABY HAS BECOME ACCUSTOMED
TO SIMPLE PURÉES, HE WILL BE READY FOR MORE
ADVENTUROUS COMBINATIONS OF FOODS. PURÉES
WITH STRONGER FLAVOURS AND THICKER TEXTURES
CAN BE INTRODUCED, AND EVEN A FEW SIMPLE
FINGER FOODS THAT ENABLE HIM TO PRACTISE
SELF-FEEDING. HE WILL BE GROWING RAPIDLY AND
HIS DIET SHOULD BE GRADUALLY ADAPTED
TO REFLECT HIS CHANGING NEEDS.

Exploring Tastes

BETWEEN 6 AND 9 MONTHS is a time of rapid development and your baby will spend many more hours awake than previously. It is a good idea to introduce plenty of new flavours, in addition to the ones he already knows. Since everything is new for him, he will be receptive to these changes. This is a stage when solids should become a fixed part of your baby's daily diet.

Moving on from purées

LEARNING TO CHEW

Every baby develops at his own pace, but your baby's first tooth (a front incisor) will probably be cut at around 6–7 months; the remaining incisors usually follow in the next 5 months. As teeth begin to emerge, you can introduce coarser textures. Your baby will mostly use his gums to chew, so mashed and finely chopped food will provide ample chewing practice. It is not a good idea to offer smooth purées for too long as your baby may become lazy about chewing and have difficulty developing the tongue movements needed to deal with real solids. If he refuses lumpy food, make the transition easier by introducing a little mashed or grated food into his usual purées, or perhaps make a favourite meal in a thicker or coarser form. Introduce wider combinations of ingredients and don't be afraid to mix sweet with savoury: fruit combined with vegetables, fish or meat often appeals to babies.

INTRODUCING COW'S MILK

You can now use cow's milk in cooking and with breakfast cereals, but formula or breast milk should remain your baby's main drink as these contain nutrients that cow's milk lacks, such as iron and vitamin D. Iron is particularly vital. Babies are born with sufficient iron reserves for the first 6 months of life, but after that, iron is required from food sources. Follow-on milks, which contain more iron than standard formulas, are designed for babies between 6 months and 2 years. Because they are more difficult to digest than ordinary formula milk, they should not be given to babies under 6 months. Up to the age of 1 year, babies should have at least 400ml (⅔ pint) of milk each day, mostly in the form of their usual breast or formula milk. Obviously this is difficult to measure precisely, especially if you are still breast-feeding. However, a portion of milk intake can come from dairy foods, such as yogurt or cheese. If you are breast-feeding, your baby will be receiving plenty of thirst-quenching foremilk (the first milk in any breast-feed). Formula-fed babies will probably need small amounts of cooled boiled water to drink as well as their usual milk, because formula milk is less thirst-quenching than breast milk.

CHEWING PRACTICE
A finger of oven-baked wholemeal toast makes a good teething rusk.

NEW FOODS FOR YOUR BABY

BREAD AND CEREALS, including wholemeal bread, rusks, wholegrain low-sugar breakfast cereals (mini wheat biscuits, porridge and hot oat cereal) can now be given. Avoid large amounts of high-fibre foods, such as high-fibre bread or bran flakes – these are too difficult for young babies to digest.

DAIRY PRODUCTS, such as pasteurized whole-milk Greek yogurt and fromage frais; cottage cheese, cream cheese and mild hard cheeses, such as Cheddar and Edam, are excellent nutrient-rich foods. Low-fat foods, such as reduced-fat spreads, are not suitable as they are too low in calories for a growing baby.

EGGS, if hard-boiled, and dishes made of well-cooked eggs, such as eggy fried bread, omelettes, frittatas or scrambled eggs, are fast to cook and nutritious. Do not serve raw or lightly cooked eggs to babies under 1 year old (there is some risk of salmonella). The white and yolk should be cooked until solid.

FISH FILLETS, such as plaice, cod, whiting or salmon, may be made into a purée with potato and courgette, or perhaps blended with homemade cheese sauce. Canned sardines or pilchards are useful sources of iron and essential fatty acids. Check all fish carefully for bones before serving.

RED MEAT, for example, lean minced beef or lamb, can be combined with sautéed onion, potato and mushrooms then finely chopped in a blender. Organic liver, which is easily digested, provides the best source of iron. Slow-cooked lamb, pork or beef casseroles make good purées.

CHICKEN is generally popular with babies because of its mild taste. Serve it chopped or puréed, casseroled or poached. It combines well with root vegetables like potato and carrot, and with fruits such as dessert apple, grapes, mango or papaya.

VEGETABLES, including onions, leeks, cabbage, kale, green beans, spinach and other leafy green vegetables, red peppers, tomatoes, sweetcorn, peas and mushrooms, greatly expand the dietary repertoire. Frozen vegetables often retain as many nutrients as fresh ones.

FRUITS, particularly mangoes, grapes (peeled, deseeded and halved), citrus and berry fruits can be served. Remove the pith from citrus fruits and sieve out seeds from berries. Use berries in small quantities as they can be indigestible. (Some babies have a strawberry allergy.)

BEANS AND PULSES are ideal for boosting meat purées, but they are especially valuable for vegetarian babies. Lentils and dried pulses (such as split peas or butter beans) are a good source of protein and iron. Tofu (soya bean curd) is a good meat alternative.

Family meals with your baby

Once your baby can support his head and upper body, you can introduce him to a highchair. As long as his back is supported, he will feel comfortable and he will enjoy being higher up and able to see what is going on around him. Put him in a safety harness so that he can't topple out, pull the chair away from the wall and put a splash mat on the floor to make cleaning up easier. Let him get used to being in the chair, wearing a bib and having a tray in front of him by giving him the chance to play there with his favourite toys. When you feed him, give him his own plastic spoon to hold. If he drinks milk from a bottle let him have that in the highchair at first. He will soon be ready to enjoy eating there.

FIRST REFUSALS

If he finds it strange at first to be fed in this new way he may even reject the food, turning his head away each time. Don't be put off by his initial refusal. Gently encourage him to feed himself, even though it is a messy business. His hand-to-eye coordination will be improving all the time and he'll soon start dipping his spoon in and out of the food and aiming it at his mouth.

JOINING IN

Even though your baby has only just begun to take solids and has many more meals than older members of the family, draw his highchair up to the table so that he can join you at meals as often as possible. He will learn that meals are sociable and fun, as well as satisfying for his stomach. Try to plan and vary his menus along the lines of the family mealtimes. For example, give him baby rice or cereal for breakfast, a savoury dish followed by pieces of fruit or cheese for lunch, and perhaps a selection of finger foods with his milk drink for supper.

EATING TOGETHER
Your baby will now be taking 2–3 tablespoons of solid food at mealtimes. You'll need to help her get most of the food to the right destination, but encourage her attempts at self-feeding.

DRINKS AT MEALTIMES

Now that solid food is beginning to replace part of your baby's milk diet at mealtimes, he will need to start drinking water to quench his thirst. It is best to start with sterile cooled boiled water rather than water straight from the tap and to avoid sweetened fruit juices or herbal drinks. Drinks with added sugar or artificial sweeteners are too sugary for babies or toddlers, and tea or coffee shouldn't be offered as they reduce iron absorption and are stimulants. On the other hand, diluted orange juice is a useful source of vitamin C and can be given from time to time. Now is the moment to introduce a beaker or training cup. These have lids in various designs, but your baby may prefer one that allows him to use the familiar sucking mechanism. Beakers with soft, flexible spouts can eventually be replaced by cups with shorter, firmer spouts, perhaps at around 8–9 months. He will still be getting most of his liquid from his usual milk and some from the purées he eats, but a cup of water that he can handle for himself at the table will allow him to choose when he wants to drink and how much.

Vegetarian meals

Parents who follow a vegetarian diet sometimes worry that this may not be suitable for their children. It is true that a bulky, high-fibre vegetarian diet is not suitable for growing young children because it is too low in calories and essential fats, and even hinders absorption of iron. However, a vegetarian diet is perfectly adequate for babies and small children as long as meals are carefully balanced. Animal proteins, including those found in egg and dairy products, are high-quality with essential amino acids. Vegetable proteins, as in beans, pulses and seeds, provide a lower quality protein and should be eaten in combination with each other or with small quantities of egg or dairy foods to provide a complete protein, for example, a lentil purée with grated cheese. You can introduce pulses such as beans or lentils, soya products and cheese at around 6 months, though babies will not need the additional protein supplied by these foods until at least 9 months because breast or formula milk provides enough for their needs. The vegetarian diet is sometimes low in iron, but vitamin C-rich products, such as diluted orange juice, greatly increase the absorption of iron from non-animal iron sources so you can gradually introduce this as a drink at mealtimes. If you intend to follow a vegan weaning plan (i.e. without dairy products or eggs), you should plan your child's diet carefully, in consultation with a doctor or paediatric nutritionist.

REMEMBER

◆ NEVER LEAVE YOUR BABY alone when he is eating. If he is in a highchair, always use a safety harness that goes around his body and clips on to the chair.

◆ NEVER FORCE YOUR BABY to eat a food he does not want or to finish a meal. Let your baby's appetite be your guide.

◆ ALLOW YOUR BABY to practise feeding himself. This will be messy, so position him away from the walls and put a splash mat or an old plastic tablecloth under his chair to make cleaning easier.

◆ EAT WITH YOUR BABY whenever possible. Try to make feeding a sociable experience from the start.

◆ DON'T GIVE CHILDREN tea or coffee as they hinder iron absorption. High-fibre cereals also interfere with iron absorption.

VEGETARIAN FINGER FOODS
When your baby begins to grasp objects, finger foods in the form of steamed vegetables, ripe fruit or cheese shapes become a useful part of her diet.

New Tastes & Textures

ONCE YOUR BABY HAS ADJUSTED TO SIMPLE PURÉES, you can begin to introduce a broader range of flavours and textures. If he has become adept at chewing he is now ready for basic finger foods, and you should gradually introduce purées with thicker or lumpier textures. You can also combine more ingredients to make interesting flavours. Don't be afraid to mix sweet with savoury: fruit with puréed chicken or fish, for example, is a favourite with many babies.

SMOOTH TEXTURES

The introduction of thicker mixtures should be gradual, beginning with familiar flavours blended with new ingredients. Keep textures smooth until your baby can cope well with chewing and swallowing.

PEACH, APPLE & STRAWBERRY PURÉE

Make this purée when peaches are in season and soft fruit is perfectly ripe and sweet. It can be mixed with baby rice for a milder taste. (See page 41 for recipe.)

PAPAYA & COTTAGE CHEESE

Creamy cottage cheese is blended with juicy papaya to make a fruity, nutritious, no-cook meal. (See page 40 for recipe.)

POTATO, LEEK & PEA PURÉE

This combination of vegetables blended with unsalted fresh stock makes a mild-tasting purée. (See page 42 for recipe.)

FOODS FOR CHEWING PRACTICE

Babies may not derive much nutritional benefit from finger foods at this stage, but these foods will give valuable chewing and biting practice. Your baby will also enjoy trying to hold foods for himself: offer him wholemeal toast strips, hard, mild cheese cut into easily grasped pieces, and low-sugar rusks.

MILD CHEESE

RUSK BISCUITS

WHOLEMEAL TOAST

NEW TEXTURES

As new teeth emerge, introduce mashed or finely chopped food to accustom your baby to chewing. Try adding just a little grated or mashed food to a smooth purée, or make his favourite purée in a lumpier form.

TOMATO & CAULIFLOWER GRATIN

This blended gratin makes a good introduction to cauliflower. Cheddar cheese and deseeded tomatoes boost the flavour. (See page 44 for recipe.)

FISH WITH CARROTS & ORANGE

This purée made with fresh white fish is bursting with useful nutrients. (See page 46 for recipe.)

FIRST CHICKEN CASSEROLE
Tender chicken breast paired with sweet root vegetables is usually popular with babies. (See page 47 for recipe.)

INSTANT NO-COOK PURÉES

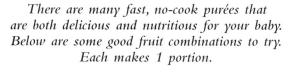

*Denotes recipes that are not suitable for freezing.

BANANA

There are many fast, no-cook purées that are both delicious and nutritious for your baby. Below are some good fruit combinations to try. Each makes 1 portion.

TIP
Always make sure that any raw fruit you give to your baby is fully ripened and sweet.

PEACH

BANANA & PEACH*
Skin and stone a small ripe peach (see page 31), then purée or mash half the flesh with half a small, ripe chopped banana.
Rich source of fibre, folate and vitamin C.

PAPAYA & COTTAGE CHEESE OR YOGURT*
Cut a small ripe papaya in half, remove the black seeds and purée or mash the flesh of one of the halves with 1 tablespoon of sieved cottage cheese or Greek yogurt. See page 38 for illustration.
Rich source of beta-carotene, protein, vitamin B12 and vitamin C.

AVOCADO

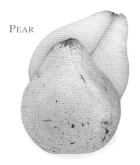

PAPAYA

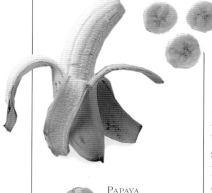

AVOCADO & BANANA OR PAPAYA*
Mash a quarter of a small avocado together with half a small ripe banana and 1–2 tablespoons of milk. You can substitute the flesh of half a papaya for the banana in this recipe – the milk is then optional.
Rich source of fibre, folate, vitamin B12, vitamin C and vitamin E.

PEAR

PLUMS

PLUM OR APRICOT & PEAR
Peel and stone a ripe apricot or plum. Slice the fruit and purée or mash the flesh with a peeled, cored and chopped soft, ripe pear.
Rich source of fibre and vitamin C.

AVOCADO & PAPAYA PURÉE

PLUM & PEAR PURÉE

MANGO & BANANA*
Purée or mash the flesh of a quarter of a small mango with half a small ripe banana.
Rich source of beta-carotene and vitamin C.

PAPAYA & CHICKEN
Cut a small ripe papaya in half, remove the black seeds and purée or mash the flesh of one of the halves with 30g (1oz) cooked boneless chicken.
Rich source of beta-carotene, fibre, protein and B vitamins.

Apricot, Pear, Peach & Apple Compôte

3 ready-to-eat dried apricots or fresh apricots

1 dessert apple, peeled, cored and chopped

1 large ripe pear, peeled, cored and chopped

1 large ripe peach or plum, peeled, stoned and chopped

For a creamier finish mix 2 tablespoons of baby rice with 4 tablespoons of milk and blend this with the fruit purée.

Simmer the fruit in a saucepan with a little water until soft, about 8–10 minutes, then blend to a purée of the desired consistency.

 Preparation/cooking
5 minutes/10 minutes

 Makes 4 portions

 Nutritional information
Rich source of fibre and vitamin C.

 Suitable for freezing

Apple, Kiwi & Pear Purée

1 dessert apple, peeled, cored and chopped

3 tbsp pure apple juice

1 ripe pear, peeled, cored and chopped

1 ripe kiwi, peeled and chopped

2 tbsp baby rice

Baby rice allows you to produce a good purée consistency, and makes a suitable ground for new flavours. Here it is mixed with vitamin-rich kiwi.

1 Put the apple in a pan with the apple juice. Cover and simmer gently for about 8 minutes. Add the pear and kiwi and continue to simmer the fruit for 3–4 minutes.

2 Blend the fruit to a purée and sieve to get rid of the kiwi's black seeds. Stir in the baby rice (no need to cook) while the purée is warm.

 Preparation/cooking
5 minutes/12 minutes

 Makes 4 portions

 Nutritional information
Rich source of fibre and vitamin C.

 Suitable for freezing

Peach, Apple & Strawberry Purée

1 dessert apple, peeled, cored and chopped

1 large ripe peach, peeled, stoned and chopped

3 large strawberries

— NOTE —
Strawberries occasionally provoke an allergic reaction in sensitive babies.

This is a delicious fruit purée to make in the summer. It can be combined with some baby rice mixed with a little milk or water.

Steam the apple for about 6 minutes, or until tender. Add the peach and strawberries to the steamer, and continue to cook for about 3 minutes. Blend the fruits to a smooth purée.

 Preparation/cooking
5 minutes/12 minutes

 Makes 4 portions

 Nutritional information
Rich source of fibre and vitamin C.

 Suitable for freezing

See page 38 for illustration.

Juicy Pear & Prune Purée

2 ripe pears, peeled, cored and chopped

2 stoned prunes, chopped

1 tbsp baby rice

This tasty combination of fresh and dried fruits is a useful source of fibre.

Simmer the fruit in a saucepan with a little water for 5 minutes. Purée to the desired consistency, using as much cooking water as needed. Sieve to get rid of the tough prune skins. Stir in the baby rice while warm.

 Preparation/cooking
5 minutes/5 minutes

 Makes 2 portions

 Nutritional information
Rich source of fibre and vitamin C.

 Suitable for freezing

DRIED APRICOTS WITH SEMOLINA

60g (2oz) ready-to-eat dried apricots

1½ tbsp semolina

175ml (6fl oz) milk

Dried apricots blend very well with semolina, and they are a concentrated source of nutrients. This purée makes an excellent breakfast.

1 Put the apricots into a small saucepan and just cover with water. Bring to the boil, then reduce the heat and simmer for about 8 minutes, or until the apricots are tender (top up with a little more water if necessary).

2 Put the semolina in a saucepan and gradually stir in the milk over a medium heat. Bring to the boil and stir for about 3 minutes, or until thickened. Combine the apricots with the semolina and blend to a purée of the desired consistency.

NOTE
Semolina is a wheat product and should not be given to babies with actual or suspected gluten intolerance.

 Cooking
12 minutes

 Makes 4 portions

 Nutritional information
Rich source of beta-carotene, fibre and vitamin B12.

 Suitable for freezing

TIP
If using frozen portions, it may be necessary to add extra milk once the purée is defrosted to thin the consistency.

BUTTERNUT SQUASH & APPLE

500g (1lb) butternut squash or pumpkin, peeled, deseeded and chopped

1 dessert apple, peeled, cored and chopped

Mixing vegetables with fruit is a good way to encourage babies to eat vegetables. Apple brings out the natural sweetness of butternut squash.

Put the butternut squash in a steamer and cook for about 7 minutes. Add the apple to the steamer and continue to cook for about 10 minutes, or until the squash is tender. Blend to a smooth purée.

VARIATION
Omit the apple and blend the cooked squash or pumpkin with a large, juicy, skinned raw peach.

 Preparation/cooking
5 minutes/17 minutes

 Makes 4 portions

 Nutritional information
Rich source of beta-carotene, fibre, folate and vitamin C.

 Suitable for freezing

POTATO, LEEK & PEA PURÉE

30g (1oz) butter

1 leek, white part only, about 60–75g (2–2½oz), washed and sliced

175g (6oz) potatoes, chopped

250ml (8fl oz) unsalted chicken stock (see page 46) or water

60g (2oz) frozen peas

Use only fresh unsalted stock for this recipe, bought or homemade. To make this purée into a delicious soup for the family, simple add extra stock and seasoning.

1 Warm the butter in a pan, add the leek and sauté until just golden, 5–6 minutes. Add the potatoes and pour over the stock. Bring to the boil, then reduce the heat, cover and simmer for 10 minutes.

2 Add the frozen peas and continue to cook for about 6 minutes, or until the vegetables are tender. Blend to a purée using a mouli or sieve.

 Preparation/cooking
5 minutes/24 minutes

 Makes 4 portions

 Nutritional information
Rich source of fibre, folate, vitamin A and vitamin C.

 Suitable for freezing

See page 38 for illustration.

TRIO OF ROOT VEGETABLES

175g (6oz) carrots, chopped

175g (6oz) potatoes, chopped

125g (4oz) parsnips or swede, chopped

── TIP ──
It's best to use a mouli or sieve to make this purée as a food processor makes cooked potato gluey.

Babies tend to love root vegetables because of their naturally sweet flavour.

1 Put the vegetables into a saucepan and just cover with boiling water. Cook over a medium heat for about 20 minutes, or until tender. Alternatively, steam them until tender.

2 Blend the vegetables to a smooth purée with about 125ml (4fl oz) of the cooking liquid, or use boiled water from the bottom of the steamer.

Preparation/cooking
5 minutes/21 minutes

Makes 6 portions

Nutritional information
Rich source of beta-carotene, fibre, folate and vitamin C.

Suitable for freezing

LENTIL & VEGETABLE PURÉE

30g (1oz) butter

125g (4oz) leeks, finely sliced

30g (1oz) celery, chopped

125g (4oz) carrots, chopped

60g (2oz) red lentils

250g (8oz) sweet potatoes, peeled and chopped

1 bay leaf

475ml (16fl oz) unsalted chicken stock (see page 46) or water

Lentils are a good source of protein. However, some babies find lentils indigestible and so they are best not given before 8 months.

1 Melt the butter in a saucepan, add the leeks and sauté for 2–3 minutes. Stir in the celery, carrots and lentils, and cook for 2 minutes more.

2 Add the sweet potatoes and bay leaf, and pour over the stock or water. Bring to the boil, then reduce the heat, cover and simmer for about 30 minutes, or until the vegetables and lentils are tender. Remove the bay leaf. Blend to a purée for 6–8 months-old babies. Older babies can eat it as it is.

Preparation/cooking
10 minutes/40 minutes

Makes 8 portions

Nutritional information
Rich source of beta-carotene, fibre, folate, protein and vitamin C.

Suitable for freezing

SPINACH, POTATO, PARSNIP & LEEK

30g (1oz) butter

1 leek, white part only, thinly sliced

250g (8oz) potatoes, chopped

125g (4oz) parsnips, chopped

300ml (½ pint) boiling water

125g (4oz) fresh spinach, washed and tough stalks removed, or 60g (2oz) frozen spinach

1 Melt the butter in a saucepan, add the leek and sauté for 2–3 minutes. Add the potatoes and parsnips, sauté for 1 minute, then pour over the boiling water. Cover and simmer for 20 minutes.

2 Add the fresh spinach leaves, if using, and continue to cook for 3–4 minutes. If using frozen spinach, cook it in a microwave or saucepan, according to package instructions, then squeeze out the excess water. Add the spinach to the potato, leek and parsnip mixture and cook for about 2 minutes.

3 Blend the vegetables to a purée of the desired consistency, adding more water to thin the purée if needed.

 Preparation/cooking
10 minutes/30 minutes

 Makes 6 portions

 Nutritional information
Rich source of beta-carotene, fibre, folate and vitamin C.

❄ **Suitable for freezing**

SWEET POTATO, CARROT & BROCCOLI

300g (10oz) sweet potatoes, peeled and chopped

1 large carrot, sliced

125g (4oz) broccoli florets

It can be a good idea to combine popular vegetables with varieties that children tend to favour a little less. In this recipe, I have used carrot and sweet potato, which babies usually love to eat, to tone down the strong flavour of broccoli.

1 Put the sweet potatoes and carrot in a steamer and cook for 10 minutes. Add the broccoli and continue to cook for about 7 minutes, or until all the vegetables are tender.

2 Blend the vegetables with 6–7 tablespoons of water from the bottom of the steamer to make a purée of the desired consistency.

 Preparation/cooking
5 minutes/18 minutes

 Makes 6 portions

 Nutritional information
Rich source of beta-carotene, fibre, folate and vitamin C.

 Suitable for freezing

TOMATO & CAULIFLOWER GRATIN

150g (5oz) cauliflower, cut into florets

30g (1oz) butter

250g (8oz) tomatoes, skinned, deseeded and roughly chopped

30g (1oz) grated Cheddar cheese

1 Put the cauliflower florets in a steamer and cook until soft, about 12 minutes.

2 Meanwhile, warm the butter in a pan, add the tomatoes and sauté until mushy. Remove from the heat and add the cheese, stirring until melted. Mix the cauliflower with the tomato and cheese sauce, then blend to the desired consistency.

VARIATION
Steam the cauliflower until soft, then blend it with 3 tablespoons of cheese sauce (see page 71 for recipe), omitting the seasoning from the sauce.

 Preparation/cooking
5 minutes/20 minutes

 Makes 4 portions

 Nutritional information
Rich source of beta-carotene, folate, protein, vitamin B12 and vitamin C.

 Suitable for freezing

See page 39 for illustration.

FILLET OF COD WITH A TRIO OF VEGETABLES

125g (4oz) potatoes, peeled and chopped

125g (4oz) carrots, sliced

125g (4oz) cod fillet, skinned

3 peppercorns, 1 bay leaf and a sprig of parsley

100ml (3½fl oz) milk

15g (½oz) butter

1 tomato, skinned, deseeded and chopped

This dish has a fairly mild taste and, because the proportion of fish to vegetables is quite small, it makes a gentle introduction to fish for your baby.

1 Put the vegetables in a saucepan and cover with water. Bring to the boil, then reduce the heat, cover and cook for 20 minutes, or until tender.

2 Meanwhile, put the fish in a pan with the peppercorns, bay leaf and parsley. Pour over the milk then poach the fish for about 5 minutes, or until it flakes easily. Strain the milk from the fish and reserve. Discard the flavourings.

3 Melt the butter in a pan, add the tomato and sauté until mushy. Flake the fish with a fork, checking carefully for bones. Drain the vegetables then add them to the fish with the tomato and 60ml (2fl oz) of the reserved milk. Blend to a purée of the desired consistency.

 Preparation/cooking
10 minutes/25 minutes

 Makes 4 portions

 Nutritional information
Rich source of beta-carotene, folate, protein, vitamin B12 and vitamin C.

 Suitable for freezing

PLAICE FILLET WITH LEEK & CHEESE SAUCE

150g (5oz) plaice fillet, skinned

3 peppercorns, 1 bay leaf and a sprig of parsley

175ml (6fl oz) milk

30g (1oz) butter

60g (2oz) leek, finely chopped

1 tbsp flour

45g (1½oz) grated Cheddar or Edam cheese

Another good way to introduce fish to your baby is to mix it with cheese sauce. Use spinach or courgette instead of leek if you prefer.

1 Put the fish in a pan with the peppercorns, herbs and milk. Bring to the boil, then simmer, covered, for 5 minutes or until the fish flakes easily. Strain the milk and reserve. Discard the flavourings. Flake the fish with a fork, checking for bones.

2 Meanwhile, melt the butter in a saucepan, add the leek and sauté until softened.

3 Stir the flour into the leek mixture to make a paste and cook for 1 minute. Gradually add the reserved milk, bring to the boil and cook, stirring, until thickened. Remove the sauce from the heat and add the cheese, stirring until melted. Purée the fish with the leek and cheese sauce.

 Preparation/cooking
5 minutes/15 minutes

 Makes 4 portions

 Nutritional information
Rich source of calcium, folate, protein, vitamin A, vitamin B6 and vitamin B12.

 Suitable for freezing

FISH WITH CARROTS & ORANGE

175g (6oz) carrots, sliced

125g (4oz) potatoes, chopped

175g (6oz) plaice fillets

juice of 1 orange

60g (2oz) grated mild Cheddar cheese

knob of butter

This purée is rich in vitamins and calcium, and bursting with flavour. Plaice is an excellent fish to choose for young babies as it has a very soft texture.

1 Put the vegetables in a pan, cover with water and boil until soft. Alternatively, place them in a steamer and cook until tender.

2 Meanwhile, place the fish in a gratin dish, pour over the orange juice, scatter over the cheese and dot with butter. Cover, leaving an air vent, and microwave on high for 3 minutes, or until the fish flakes easily. Alternatively, cover with foil and cook in the preheated oven for about 20 minutes.

3 Flake the fish with a fork, checking for bones. Add the vegetables to the fish and its juices then blend to a purée of the desired consistency.

 Preparation/cooking
5 minutes/20 minutes

 Oven temperature
microwave on high or conventional oven at 180°C/350°F/gas 4

 Makes 6 portions

 Nutritional information
Rich source of beta-carotene, calcium, folate, protein, vitamin B6 and vitamin B12.

 Suitable for freezing

See page 39 for illustration.

GRANDMA'S CHICKEN SOUP & STOCK

1 large boiler chicken with giblets, cut into 8 pieces and trimmed of excess fat, or 1 roast chicken carcass, broken up

2.5 litres (4 pints) water

2 large onions, roughly chopped

3 large carrots, roughly sliced

2 parsnips, roughly chopped

2 leeks, sliced

1 celery stalk

2 sprigs of parsley

2 or 3 chicken stock-cubes (for babies over 1 year)

I use fresh chicken stock as the base for many of my recipes. This makes a delicious soup for older family members if it is fortified with tiny soup pasta or vermicelli and enriched with stock-cubes.

1 Put the raw or cooked chicken pieces into a very large pan and cover with the water. Slowly bring to the boil and skim off any scum that comes to the surface.

2 Add all the remaining ingredients, including the stock-cubes if making it for older children. Cover and simmer gently for about 2 hours, checking it occasionally and adding more water as necessary. Remove the chicken pieces. If you have used boiler chicken, strip off the flesh and set aside. Return the bones to the pan and cook for another hour.

3 Remove the pan from the heat and allow to cool. Chill for at least 4 hours or overnight, then skim off the layer of fat from the surface.

4 Strain the stock through a sieve into a clean pan or bowl. If desired, you can make a purée by blending a little of the stock together with some of the cooked vegetables and pieces of chicken.

 Preparation/cooking
10 minutes plus 4 hours refrigeration/2 hours

 Makes 1.85 litres (3 pints)

 Suitable for freezing

— TIP —
As a short-cut, make your own stock from the left-over carcass of a roast chicken, adding giblets, if available, and perhaps a veal marrow bone from the butcher for extra flavour.

— NOTE —
Do not use stock-cubes or paste in food for babies under 1 year as these products contain large amounts of salt.

FIRST CHICKEN CASSEROLE

1 tbsp vegetable oil

100g (3½oz) carrots, chopped

60g (2oz) leeks, white part only, sliced

75g (2½oz) chicken breast, cut into chunks

250g (8oz) potatoes, chopped

75g (2½oz) parsnips, chopped

Babies tend to like the mild taste of chicken. Here I have combined it with vegetables that have a naturally sweet taste. Root vegetables are also good as they help to give a smooth texture.

1 Warm the oil in a pan, add the carrots and leeks and sauté until softened, about 6 minutes. Add the chicken and sauté, turning occasionally, until sealed.

2 Add the potatoes and parsnips and just cover with boiling water. Cover and simmer for about 15 minutes, or until everything is tender and cooked through. Blend to a purée, or leave chopped for older babies.

 Preparation/cooking
10 minutes/22 minutes

 Makes 6 portions

 Nutritional information
Rich source of beta-carotene, folate, protein and vitamin A.

Suitable for freezing

See page 39 for illustration.

TASTY MINCED MEAT WITH SWEDE & TOMATO

½ tbsp vegetable oil

30g (1oz) onion, finely chopped

125g (4oz) lean minced beef

125g (4oz) organic chicken livers (optional)

250g (8oz) swede, chopped

2 tomatoes, skinned, deseeded and chopped

250ml (8fl oz) unsalted chicken stock (see page 46) or beef stock

This makes a good introduction to minced meat as it has a nice soft texture and a natural sweetness provided by the swede.

1 Heat the oil in a frying pan, add the onion and sauté until softened. Add the minced beef and chicken livers, if using, and sauté, stirring occasionally, until browned.

2 Add the swede and tomatoes, pour over the stock, holding back a little if a thicker consistency is preferred, and bring to the boil. Reduce the heat, cover and cook for 30 minutes. Blend to a purée of the desired consistency.

 Preparation/cooking
10 minutes/40 minutes

 Makes 8 portions

 Nutritional information
Rich source of folate, protein, vitamin B12 and zinc.

 Suitable for freezing

BRAISED BEEF WITH CARROT, PARSNIP & POTATO

30g (1oz) butter

125g (4oz) leeks, sliced

175g (6oz) lean beef stewing steak, cut into cubes

150g (5oz) carrots, sliced

125g (4oz) parsnips, chopped

250g (8oz) potatoes, chopped

450ml (¾ pint) unsalted beef stock or chicken stock (see opposite)

This combination of root vegetables and beef has a smooth consistency that appeals to young babies.

1 Heat the butter in a flame-proof casserole, add the leeks and sauté for 5 minutes, or until softened. Add the beef and sauté until browned.

2 Add the carrots, parsnips and potatoes to the casserole, pour over the stock and bring the mixture to the boil.

3 Transfer the casserole to the preheated oven and cook for 1½–2 hours, or until the meat is soft. Blend to a purée of the desired consistency.

 Preparation/cooking
10 minutes/1¾–2¼ hours

 Oven temperature
180°C/350°F/gas 4

 Makes 10 portions

 Nutritional information
Rich source of beta-carotene, folate, niacin, protein, vitamin B1, vitamin B12 and zinc.

 Suitable for freezing

9-12
Months

SOLID FOODS SHOULD NOW BE THE
FOCUS OF YOUR CHILD'S MEALS. THIS IS A
TIME OF GROWING INDEPENDENCE AND YOUR
BABY MAY INSIST ON FEEDING HERSELF. SHE WILL
PROBABLY BE MUCH MORE PROFICIENT AT
CHEWING NOW, AND CHOPPED OR MASHED FOOD
CAN REPLACE PURÉES. FOODS FROM PREVIOUS
CHAPTERS CAN STILL BE SERVED TO HER; SIMPLY
ADJUST THE TEXTURE AS NECESSARY.

Growing Appetites

As SHE APPROACHES her first birthday, your baby will experience a broader range of foods, and will have started to transfer her allegiance from milk to "grown-up" meals. Her increasing sense of autonomy will show itself in her change from a passive eater to an active eater as she enjoys trying to feed herself. This process may seem more like a messy sort of play to you, but it is important to give young children freedom to explore their food.

Exploring texture

At this age, your baby may well be on the way to eating three main meals a day, so that she receives a combination of starchy food, vegetable or animal protein, and fruit or vegetables. She will manage coarser textures (see pages 54–55), especially with the arrival of teeth to improve her chewing abilities (see page 52). She can master finger foods (see opposite), so keep up her energy levels between meals with healthy snacks of sandwiches or fruit slices. Her diet can now include virtually all the foods the rest of the family eats, except lightly cooked eggs, nuts, shellfish, unpasteurized or soft cheese, and low-fat or high-fibre products. Indeed, many dishes can be shared by all the family as long as your baby's portion is unseasoned.

KEEPING UP HER MILK

Your baby may be drinking less milk as her appetite for solid food increases, but she still needs 400ml (⅔ pint) of her usual breast or formula milk per day (see page 34). If your baby has used bottles, aim to decrease their use gradually so you can dispense with them altogether during the coming weeks. It helps if you give most milk-feeds in a beaker or cup, perhaps reserving a soothing bottle-feed for bedtime.

HYGIENE

Once your baby is 10 months old and actively exploring her environment (which often involves her "tasting" every object she lays her hands upon), there seems little point in sterilizing feeding spoons. However, bottles, teats and beaker spouts should be thoroughly washed and sterilized until she is 1 year old. Your baby's hands should also be washed before and after eating. This is particularly important now that she is probably using her hands to dip into her meals as well as for picking up finger foods.

MANUAL SKILLS
Your baby can now manage food with a lumpier texture and she'll pick out some of the pieces herself to pop in her mouth.

New independence

Your baby is now acquiring new physical skills: rolling, crawling, sitting or even walking. Improved muscle power and hand-to-eye coordination skills allow her much more independent movement. Your baby will be delighted by the freedom her body is giving her and she will want to take the lead at mealtimes by feeding herself; she may even become impatient when you try to spoon-feed her, and prefer to be helped with just the odd spoonful of food. She will probably be following a more predictable sleeping pattern, which helps to regulate mealtimes.

ENCOURAGING SELF-FEEDING
Your baby will need progressively less help to eat, and may well prefer to spoon soft foods up for herself. If more purée seems to go

on the floor or her lap than in her mouth, you could use a two-spoon system: give her a spoon to hold so that she can make her own attempts at self-feeding, and use another spoon yourself to get some of the food to her mouth.

FINGER FOODS
Finger foods are excellent for teaching self-feeding and should begin to play a useful part in her diet; she will enjoy the freedom of movement they give her, and will appreciate the fact that she can eat this kind of food without adult intervention. Let her try steamed or raw vegetable sticks with a cold dip, or a favourite purée with bread sticks as finger foods. Remember that finger foods should be firm enough for your baby to pick up, yet tender enough for her to chew and

swallow easily. Just because your baby has teeth, it doesn't mean that she instinctively knows how to use them for chewing: young babies are quite likely to bite off a piece of food, try to swallow it whole and choke, so they must not be left unsupervised when eating, even for a moment.

EXPERIMENTATION
The more you allow your baby to experiment, the quicker she will learn to feed herself. It may be a messy procedure, but you should not discourage her attempts, or worry that her table manners are less than perfect. She will be quick to pick up any anxieties on your part and could soon turn mealtimes into a battleground. Allow her to explore the feel of the food and take her time over eating it.

He has fine-tuned his grip and is well on the way to independent feeding

PRACTICE
A suction-based bowl keeps the food in one place while he makes a studied attempt to load his spoon and bring it to his mouth without dropping it.

PERFECTION
Once he has learned to manoeuvre the spoon correctly, his confidence will grow and he will probably proudly resist all offers of assistance.

Teething

During the 3 months leading up to your baby's first birthday, she may cut several teeth so it is still important to offer textured foods that will encourage her to chew. If vegetable finger foods are cooled in the fridge first they will be especially soothing on her gums. Opinions differ as to how far teething affects a baby's well-being, but it is probable that teething could cause her some distress, and even make her fussier than usual about her food. For a few days before each tooth breaks through the gum, you may notice a hard, whitish bump under the surface of the gum. She might dribble, so it is a good idea to put a little petroleum jelly around her mouth and chin to help prevent it becoming dry and red. If her gums are particularly tender, she may reject being fed from a spoon, so offer her finger foods to eat instead.

DENTAL HYGIENE

Start brushing your baby's teeth as soon as they appear – at least twice a day, in the morning and at bedtime. Make toothbrushing fun, perhaps by giving your baby her own toothbrush to hold while you brush your teeth. Bend down and show her what you are doing and encourage her to copy you. Of course, she won't manage a proper clean, but it will give her the right idea.

GEL-FILLED   VEGETABLE STICKS
TEETHING RING

COOLING SORE GUMS
Vegetable sticks, such as cucumber and carrot, can be chilled in the refrigerator and offered to your baby to bite on. Alternatively, cool a teething ring in the fridge for him to bite on.

PREVENTING DECAY

For most children a mild-tasting fluoride toothpaste (varieties for children have a slightly lower fluoride content) and a good diet are sufficient to protect teeth. Avoid gimmicky flavoured toothpaste since it is more helpful in the long run for children to know the difference between the taste of bubble gum and the taste of conventional toothpaste. To limit the possibility of tooth decay, never fill bottles with anything but milk or water: that way you prevent prolonged contact of sugary or acidic fluids with the teeth and gums. However, milk itself does contain a form of sugar that could be corrosive if the teeth were never cleaned. Once your baby's teeth have been brushed at bedtime, don't give her sweet drinks or more food because at night there is not enough saliva in the mouth to wash away harmful acid.

TEETHING FOODS
When he is teething, finger foods may be more appealing for your baby than eating from a spoon. However, don't be tempted to leave him to chew on food alone; he is still at risk of choking on small pieces of food.

Iron and growth

Babies are born with sufficient iron for the first six months of life, but after that they need to derive an adequate amount from their daily diet. Iron deficiency is in fact one of the most common nutritional problems in the world.

IRON DEFICIENCY

Iron deficiency can be difficult to spot as the physical symptoms are not so readily identifiable as those of an infectious illness. If symptoms of pallor, listlessness and fatigue are missed, it can lead to anaemia, which in turn results in poor energy levels. However, it should not be difficult to prevent this problem occurring, or to eliminate it, by providing adequate dietary sources of iron.

DIETARY SOURCES OF IRON

Iron in foods of animal origin, such as red meat, particularly liver, or oily fish (salmon, sardines, mackerel or pilchards, for example), is much more easily absorbed than iron in foods of plant origin (see below for examples of iron-rich foods). However, if you include a good source of vitamin C at the same meal as a plant-based source of iron, you can improve the absorption of the iron. For example, a beaker of fresh orange juice, slices of kiwi fruit, a few chunks of sweet red pepper, or cauliflower florets are all vitamin C-rich foods and could be served at the same meal as a spinach or lentil dish. This would enable the iron in the latter to be better absorbed. Protein-rich foods also aid iron absorption. By mixing fish, lean red meat or chicken with dark green leafy vegetables or lentils, you will improve the absorption of the vegetable sources of iron by about three times.

REMEMBER

♦ DO NOT OFFER your baby nuts, raw or lightly cooked eggs, soft or unpasteurized cheeses or shellfish.

♦ HONEY SHOULD NOT be given to babies under the age of 1 as in rare cases it can contain bacteria that cause botulism. However, if it is an ingredient in processed food, it is perfectly safe.

♦ ENCOURAGE YOUR BABY to drink from a cup or beaker, and offer only water, diluted juice or her usual milk.

♦ OFFER FINGER FOODS as part of your baby's meals to give her chewing practice and encourage her to feed independently.

♦ AS SOON AS teeth appear, buy a mild toothpaste designed for children and brush your baby's teeth morning and night.

♦ DON'T OFFER tea, coffee or cola drinks to your baby.

TOP IRON-RICH FOODS

LIVER AND RED MEATS

EGG YOLK (MUST BE WELL-COOKED FOR BABIES)

OILY FISH, FRESH OR CANNED (CHECK FOR BONES)

PULSES, SUCH AS LENTILS AND BAKED BEANS

BREAKFAST CEREALS FORTIFIED WITH IRON

BREAD AND RUSKS

GREEN LEAFY VEGETABLES, SUCH AS SPINACH AND CABBAGE

DRIED FRUITS, ESPECIALLY APRICOTS

A Varied Menu

TOWARDS THE END of your baby's first year, solid food will replace much of her milk diet. It is important to introduce lots of different textures and flavours while your baby is so receptive to new foods. Offer some food mashed, some whole, some grated and some diced: it's surprising what a few teeth and strong gums can manage. Finger foods that allow your baby to feed herself will become an increasingly important part of the daily diet, and will accustom her to many new textures.

QUICK CHICKEN COUSCOUS

Couscous, which is made from crushed semolina, has a mild taste and soft texture that is perfect for babies. It is also very quick to cook and combines well with a variety of vegetables and even fruit. (See page 60 for recipe.)

CHEESY PASTA STARS

Tiny stars or other soup pasta shapes make an ideal introduction to pasta. Here they are combined with a tomato sauce enriched with grated Cheddar and sweetened with carrot. (See page 58 for recipe.)

FINGER FOODS

All finger foods should be firm enough for your baby to pick up, yet tender enough for her to chew and swallow easily. These foods are perfect for encouraging your child to feed independently, but never leave her alone while she is eating.

Chewing on chilled cucumber pieces may soothe sore gums

Toast shapes give good chewing practice

CREAMY AVOCADO DIP

This dip combines buttery, creamy-textured avocado with soft cream cheese. Serve with steamed vegetable shapes, such as sweet potato, or crunchy vegetable sticks and cheese or bread shapes.

(See page 56 for recipe.)

Cut cheese into novelty shapes

Offer soft pitta bread strips and crunchy bread sticks

RED PEPPER DIP

This colourful purée of roasted red pepper, tomato and cream cheese is served with raw vegetable sticks, which may be chilled to soothe gums made sore by teething.
(See page 56 for recipe.)

Sweet, ripe, raw slices of apple and strawberry are excellent finger foods

RASPBERRY, PEAR & PEACH PURÉE

A mixture of a purée of sweet, ripe fruits with mild, thick, natural yogurt makes a delicious summery dip. Offer raw fruit slices for dunking.
(See page 57 for recipe.)

CREAMY AVOCADO DIP & VEGETABLE FINGERS

1 ripe avocado, halved and stoned

60g (2oz) soft cream cheese

1 tbsp snipped chives

1 tomato, skinned, deseeded and chopped

STEAMED VEGETABLE SHAPES

vegetables such as sweet potato, carrot, potato and parsnip, washed and peeled

An avocado has the highest protein content of any fruit, and babies like its mild creaminess. This dip also makes a good sandwich filling if mixed with grated cheese or chopped watercress.

1 Cut the vegetables into sticks or shapes, place in a steamer and cook until tender, about 8 minutes.

2 Scoop out the avocado flesh. Mash until smooth and mix with the remaining ingredients. (For adults you can add lemon juice, seasoning, chopped coriander and maybe a little finely chopped chilli.)

 Preparation/cooking
10 minutes/8 minutes

 Makes 4 portions

 Nutritional information
Rich source of folate, vitamin A, vitamin C and vitamin E.

See page 55 for illustration.

RED PEPPER DIP & VEGETABLE FINGERS

1 small red pepper, halved and deseeded

½ tbsp vegetable oil

1 shallot, peeled and finely chopped

1 ripe tomato, skinned, deseeded and chopped

200g (7oz) cream cheese

RAW VEGETABLE SHAPES

vegetables such as carrot, celery, cucumber, pepper and kohlrabi, washed and peeled

The vegetables for this dip should be cut into pieces small enough to be easily grasped, but not so tiny that they could be swallowed whole. You can also offer toast, pitta fingers or mild cheese shapes.

1 To make the dip, roast the red pepper, then peel and roughly chop.

2 Meanwhile, warm the oil in a small frying pan, add the shallot and sauté until softened but not coloured. Combine the red pepper with the shallot, tomato and cream cheese, and blend together to make a smooth cream.

3 Cut the raw vegetables into strips, or make novelty shapes using miniature biscuit cutters.

 Preparation/cooking
10 minutes/10 minutes

 Makes 4 portions

 Nutritional information
Rich source of beta-carotene, vitamin B12 and vitamin C.

See page 55 for illustration.

—— TIP ——
If your baby finds raw vegetables too hard, offer steamed cauliflower or root vegetables (see above). Reduce the steaming time progressively.

EASY MASHED VEGETABLE DUO

250g (8oz) swede, chopped

125g (4oz) parsnips, chopped

250ml (8fl oz) milk

30g (1oz) grated Cheddar cheese

This recipe makes both a good smooth purée and a slightly coarser textured dish, as preferred.

Place the vegetables in a saucepan with the milk. Bring to the boil, cover and simmer for 20 minutes, or until soft. Remove from the heat and stir in the cheese until melted. Mash to the desired consistency.

 Preparation/cooking
10 minutes/22 minutes

 Makes 4 portions

 Nutritional information
Rich source of calcium, folate, vitamin A, vitamin B12 and vitamin C.

❄ Suitable for freezing

FRUITY BABY MUESLI

30g (1oz) rolled oats

30g (1oz) toasted wheatgerm

1 dried apricot or pear, chopped

1 tbsp sultanas

150ml (¼ pint) white grape juice or apple juice

½ red apple, peeled and grated

3 grapes, halved and deseeded

Oats raise blood sugar relatively slowly, so oat-based breakfast cereals provide a more sustained energy boost than other cereals.

1 Put the oats and wheatgerm in a bowl with the dried apricot and sultanas. Pour over the grape juice. Leave to soak for at least 2 hours or overnight.

2 Add the apple and grapes to the soaked cereal and blend. (Once your baby has mastered the art of chewing, there is no need to blend this muesli.)

Preparation
10 minutes, plus
2–12 hours soaking

Makes 2 portions

Nutritional information
Rich source of fibre, iron, B vitamins, vitamin C and zinc.

APPLE & DATE PORRIDGE

1 dessert apple, peeled, cored and chopped

45g (1½oz) dates

4 tbsp water

150ml (¼ pint) milk

15g (½oz) rolled oats

1 Put the apple and dates in a pan with the water and cook over a medium heat for 5 minutes.

2 Meanwhile, heat the milk in a pan, stir in the oats, bring to the boil and simmer, stirring constantly, for 3–4 minutes, or until thickened. Mix with the fruit, then blend to the desired consistency.

Preparation/cooking
2 minutes/12 minutes

Makes 2 portions

Nutritional information
Rich source of calcium, folate and vitamin B12.

EXOTIC FRUIT SALAD

½ mango, peeled and stoned

½ papaya, peeled and stoned

1 kiwi fruit, peeled

2 lychees, peeled and stoned

juice of 1 large orange

If you can't find perfectly ripe, sweet exotic fruits, substitute peaches or strawberries.

Finely chop all the fruit and simply combine with the orange juice.

Preparation
10 minutes

Makes 4 portions

Nutritional information
Rich source of beta-carotene and vitamin C.

RASPBERRY, PEAR & PEACH PURÉE

125g (4oz) raspberries

2 ripe pears, peeled, cored and chopped

1 peach, skinned and chopped

2 tbsp Greek yogurt

See page 55 for illustration.

This is very much a summer purée: to be made when raspberries and peaches are ripe and sweet. It is also good mixed with baby rice or mashed banana.

Place the fruits in a saucepan and simmer gently for about 5 minutes. Cool slightly, press through a sieve and mix with the yogurt.

Preparation/cooking
5 minutes/10 minutes

Makes 4 portions

Nutritional information
Rich source of fibre, folate and vitamin C.

Suitable for freezing

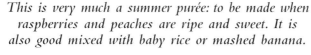

BUTTERNUT SQUASH WITH ALPHABET PASTA

300g (10oz) butternut squash, peeled and cubed

2–3 tbsp alphabet soup pasta

30g (1oz) butter

½ tbsp chopped fresh sage

1 Put the squash in a steamer and cook until tender, about 15 minutes. Blend to a purée with 4–5 tablespoons of water from the bottom of the steamer.

2 Meanwhile, bring a pan of water to the boil, add the pasta and cook until tender, about 5 minutes, then drain. Melt the butter in a pan, add the sage and cook gently for 1 minute. Mix the sage butter with the squash and pasta.

 Preparation/cooking
5 minutes/20 minutes

 Makes 4 portions

 Nutritional information
Rich source of beta-carotene, folate and vitamin C.

 Suitable for freezing

CHEESY PASTA STARS

125g (4oz) carrots, sliced

200ml (7fl oz) boiling water

30g (1oz) butter

200g (7oz) tomatoes, skinned, deseeded and chopped

45g (1½oz) grated Cheddar cheese

2 tbsp soup pasta stars (stelline)

Tiny pasta stelline make a good introduction to pasta. The sweet taste of the carrots in this sauce is usually very appealing to babies.

1 Place the carrots in a small pan, cover with the boiling water and cook until tender, 15–20 minutes. Warm the butter in a separate pan, add the tomatoes and sauté until mushy. Remove from the heat and stir in the cheese until melted.

2 Meanwhile, bring a pan of water to the boil, add the pasta and cook until tender, about 5 minutes, then drain.

3 Mix together the cooked carrots with their cooking liquid and the cheese and tomato sauce. Blend to a purée then combine with the pasta stars.

 Preparation/cooking
10 minutes/25 minutes

 Makes 4 portions

 Nutritional information
Rich source of beta-carotene, calcium, folate, protein, vitamin B12 and vitamin C.

 Suitable for freezing

See page 54 for illustration.

TOMATO & MASCARPONE PASTA SAUCE

1 tbsp olive oil

1 shallot, finely chopped

1 garlic clove, crushed

400g (13oz) canned chopped tomatoes

1 tbsp tomato purée

1 tsp balsamic vinegar

½ tsp sugar

½ tsp mixed herbs

3 tbsp mascarpone cheese

Mascarpone is an Italian fresh cream cheese. This sauce goes well with pasta and is also good served with chicken. To adapt the sauce for adults, I would add a little chopped red chilli at the same time as the shallot and garlic, and season to taste with salt and freshly ground black pepper.

1 Heat the oil in a saucepan, add the shallot and garlic and sauté for 2 minutes.

2 Add the remaining ingredients except the mascarpone and cook over a medium heat for about 15 minutes.

3 Purée the sauce in a blender and stir in the mascarpone cheese.

 Preparation/cooking
5 minutes/20 minutes

 Makes 4 portions

 Nutritional information
Rich source of folate.

 Suitable for freezing

FILLET OF FISH MORNAY WITH VEGETABLES

15g (½oz) butter

60g (2oz) leeks, finely sliced

125g (4oz) carrots, chopped

60g (2oz) broccoli, cut into small florets

45g (1½oz) fresh or frozen peas

150g (5oz) cod, hake, plaice or haddock fillets, skinned

150ml (¼ pint) milk

3 peppercorns, 1 bay leaf and a sprig of parsley

20g (¾oz) butter

1 tbsp plain flour

45g (1½oz) grated Cheddar or Edam cheese

This tasty combination of white fish and vegetables in a mild cheese sauce is generally very popular with babies.

1 Melt the butter in a saucepan, add the leeks and sauté for 2–3 minutes. Add the carrots, cover with water and cook for 10 minutes. Add the broccoli and cook for 5 minutes. Stir in the peas and simmer for a further 5 minutes, or until the vegetables are tender (adding a little more water if necessary).

2 Meanwhile, put the fish in a pan with the milk, peppercorns, bay leaf and parsley. Simmer for 5 minutes, or until the fish is cooked. Set aside, reserving the cooking liquid. Discard the flavourings.

3 To prepare the sauce, melt the butter in a pan, stir in the flour and cook for 1 minute. Gradually whisk in the fish cooking liquid, bring to the boil and cook until the sauce has thickened. Remove from the heat, add the cheese and stir until melted.

4 Drain the vegetables and mix with the flaked fish and cheese sauce. Blend to a purée of the desired consistency for young babies. Provided the vegetables are tender, this can be mashed or chopped for older babies who are starting to chew.

 Preparation/cooking
10 minutes/35 minutes

 Makes 8 portions

 Nutritional information
Rich source of beta-carotene, calcium, folate, protein, vitamin B6, vitamin B12 and vitamin C.

 Suitable for freezing

Flaked Cod with Tomatoes & Courgettes

150g (5oz) cod fillet, skinned

100ml (3½fl oz) milk

30g (1oz) butter

1 shallot, chopped

90g (3oz) courgettes, chopped

375g (12oz) tomatoes, skinned, deseeded and chopped

60g (2oz) grated Cheddar cheese

1 Place the fish in a saucepan, cover with the milk and poach gently for about 6 minutes.

2 Meanwhile, melt the butter in a pan, add the shallot and cook until softened. Add the courgettes and sauté for 5 minutes. Add the tomatoes and sauté for 5 minutes more, or until mushy. Remove from the heat and stir in the cheese until melted.

3 Flake the fish carefully, checking for bones, and stir it into the tomato and courgette sauce. For babies who don't yet like lumpy food, blend the mixture to a smoother consistency.

 Preparation/cooking
10 minutes/20 minutes

 Makes 4 portions

 Nutritional information
Rich source of beta-carotene, calcium, folate, protein, vitamin B6, vitamin B12 and vitamin C.

 Suitable for freezing

TIP
The cod can be microwaved on a high setting for 3 minutes.

California Chicken

45g (1½oz) cooked chicken

1 tomato, skinned, deseeded and chopped

30g (1oz) avocado

2 tbsp mild natural yogurt

1½ tbsp grated Cheddar cheese

Use these ingredients to make yourself a salad or sandwich at the same time as a quick and easy meal for your baby. You can substitute Edam for Cheddar cheese.

Chop the chicken, then combine it with the remaining ingredients. Blend the mixture to the desired consistency.

 Preparation
10 minutes

 Makes 1 portion

 Nutritional information
Rich source of calcium, folate, protein, vitamin A, B vitamins, vitamin C, vitamin E and zinc.

Quick Chicken Couscous

20g (¾oz) butter

60g (2oz) leeks, finely chopped

60g (2oz) chicken, diced

30g (1oz) parsnips, diced

30g (1oz) carrots, diced

250ml (8fl oz) unsalted chicken stock (see page 46)

100g (3½oz) couscous

If you prefer, replace the chicken with extra seasonal vegetables.

1 Warm the butter in a pan, add the leeks and sauté for 5 minutes, or until softened. Add the chicken and sauté until just cooked through.

2 Meanwhile, place the parsnips and carrots in a steamer, or in a saucepan with boiling water to cover, and cook until tender, about 10 minutes.

3 Bring the stock to the boil in a pan. Stir in the couscous, remove from the heat, cover and leave for 5 minutes, or until the stock has been absorbed. Fluff with a fork and stir in the chicken and vegetables. Add extra stock or water if necessary.

 Preparation/cooking
10 minutes/20 minutes

 Makes 4 portions

 Nutritional information
Rich source of beta-carotene, folate, iron and protein.

See page 54 for illustration.

FRUITY CHICKEN WITH CARROTS

15g (½oz) butter

30g (1oz) onion, finely chopped

75g (2½oz) boneless, skinless chicken, chopped

125g (4oz) carrots, sliced

½ dessert apple, peeled, cored and chopped

150ml (¼ pint) unsalted chicken stock (see page 46)

Apple blends well with chicken to produce a lovely flavour in this quick-to-prepare dish. Well-cooked rice makes a good accompaniment.

1 Heat the butter in a pan, add the onion and sauté for 3–4 minutes. Add the chicken and sauté until it turns opaque. Add the carrots and cook for 2 minutes then stir in the chopped apple and pour over the chicken stock.

2 Bring the mixture to the boil, then cover and cook over a medium heat for about 15 minutes. Chop or purée to the desired consistency.

 Preparation/cooking
10 minutes/22 minutes

 Makes 4 portions

 Nutritional information
Rich source of beta-carotene, niacin, protein and vitamin B6.

 Suitable for freezing

CREAMY CHICKEN & BROCCOLI

90g (3oz) broccoli, cut into small florets

125g (4oz) cooked chicken, chopped

MILD CHEESE SAUCE

30g (1oz) butter

2 tbsp plain flour

300ml (½ pint) milk

60g (2oz) grated Edam or other mild cheese

You could add some small cooked soup pasta, such as stelline, to this recipe to make it more substantial.

1 To prepare the cheese sauce, melt the butter in a saucepan, stir in the flour and cook for 1 minute. Gradually whisk in the milk, bring to the boil and cook until the sauce has thickened. Remove from the heat, add the cheese and stir until melted.

2 Meanwhile, steam or microwave the broccoli until tender. Combine the cheese sauce, chicken and broccoli then roughly chop the mixture in a blender or by hand.

 Preparation/cooking
5 minutes/15 minutes

 Makes 4 portions

 Nutritional information
Rich source of calcium, folate, niacin, protein, vitamin A, vitamin B6, vitamin B12 and vitamin C.

 Suitable for freezing

TIP
If your baby isn't keen on cheese, make a white sauce flavoured with a pinch of nutmeg.

BABY'S BOLOGNESE

1 tbsp vegetable oil

30g (1oz) onion, finely chopped

15g (½oz) celery, finely chopped

30g (1oz) carrots, finely grated

125g (4oz) lean minced beef

½ tsp tomato purée

2 tomatoes, skinned, deseeded and chopped

90ml (3fl oz) unsalted chicken stock (see page 46)

45g (1½oz) spaghetti

1 Warm the oil in a pan, add the onion and celery and sauté for 3–4 minutes. Add the grated carrots and cook for 2 minutes.

2 Add the minced beef and stir until browned. Stir in the tomato purée, tomatoes and stock. Bring the mixture to the boil, reduce the heat, cover and cook for 10–15 minutes, or until the meat is cooked through.

3 Meanwhile, bring a pan of water to the boil, add the spaghetti and cook until soft, about 10 minutes. Drain and chop into small pieces. Transfer the bolognese sauce to a blender and purée to a fairly smooth, uniform texture before combining it with the pasta.

 Preparation/cooking
10 minutes/35 minutes

 Makes 6 portions

 Nutritional information
Rich source of beta-carotene, folate, niacin, protein, vitamin B12 and zinc.

 Suitable for freezing
Sauce only

TIP
Babies sometimes find the chewy texture of red meat off-putting so I like to purée this sauce in a blender before serving.

12-18
Months

YOUR CHILD CAN NOW ENJOY A FULL, VARIED DIET AND IT SHOULD BE EASIER TO INTEGRATE HIM INTO FAMILY MEALS. ACCORDINGLY, THE RECIPES IN THIS CHAPTER ARE DESIGNED TO APPEAL TO YOUR TODDLER, BUT ALSO SUIT THE TASTES OF THE WHOLE FAMILY. YOU MAY WELL FIND THAT YOUR CHILD NEEDS QUICK, ENERGY-BOOSTING SNACKS AND SO THERE ARE MANY SUGGESTIONS FOR HEALTHY SNACKS IN THIS AND THE FOLLOWING CHAPTERS.

Changing Needs

YOUR BABY IS BECOMING MOBILE and will seem to have boundless energy. By now, he can enjoy the varied mixed diet that ensures an adequate supply of the nutrients essential for his growth and energies. However, young children's individual dietary needs vary considerably at this stage: some seem to consume vast quantities of food; others thrive on surprisingly little.

Balancing a mixed diet

At around 12 months old, your baby may look quite chubby, but once he gets up on his feet, he will slim down. Once he is fully mobile, he will need snacks between meals to fuel his energy. As long as you encourage him to eat a variety of snacks, such as fruit, bites of cheese or home-made cake, they will make up a useful part of his mixed diet.

CHILDREN'S NUTRITION
Although your child will be joining in with family meals, the dietary advice that applies to you as an adult will not necessarily be appropriate for him. Young children have different nutritional needs and require enough calories to sustain the growth of muscle, tissue and bone that takes place during childhood. Advice concerning adult fat and fibre intake, for example, does not apply to the under 5s. While health experts tell us that adults and children over 5 should derive no more than 30 per cent of their calories from fat, they also agree that we should not limit fat in the

diets of children under 2. Due to the very fast rate of growth in the first 2 years of life, fat is needed as it is the most concentrated source of energy. Without enough fat in the diet, a child would need to burn up protein for energy. Fat is also important for healthy development of the brain and nervous system. Unless you have been advised by a doctor to do so, don't give your child reduced fat products, such as semi-skimmed milk. In fact, your child still needs about 400ml (⅔ pint) of milk a day, though now he can come off breast or formula milk and drink full-fat cow's milk (see opposite). A high–fibre diet, too, is still not appropriate for your child. Young children have small stomachs: fibre is low-calorie bulky material that fills the stomach without meeting a toddler's high calorific needs, and it can even hinder absorption of vital nutrients.

MILK INTAKE
Encourage your child to drink milk from a beaker or open cup, rather than a bottle. However, she doesn't always need milk; water is a much better thirst-quencher.

KEEPING MILK IN THE DIET

If your child drinks milk only reluctantly and you are worried that he is not taking the recommended 400ml (⅔ pint) of milk per day, you can easily smuggle milk into his meals. Yogurts, fromage frais or pasteurized cheese can be used as equivalents. Alternatively, offer a fruity milkshake (see page 98), make a cheese sauce (see page 71) for part of the main meal, mash some potatoes with plenty of milk, or whip a half-set jelly with a tin of evaporated milk.

DAIRY PRODUCTS IN THE DIET

FROMAGE FRAIS OR YOGURTS

CHEESE, SLICED, GRATED ON PASTA OR ON TOAST

WHITE SAUCE IN FISH PIE OR MACARONI CHEESE

MILK PUDDINGS, LIKE RICE PUDDING OR GROUND RICE

HIGH-QUALITY DAIRY ICE-CREAM

FRUITY OR CHOCOLATE MILKSHAKES

A healthy eating plan for life

Health experts recommend we all try to include five portions of fruit or vegetables (not including potatoes) in our diet each day. It is believed that this helps to protect against certain forms of cancer and heart disease, and provides the correct balance of nutrients. If you start your baby on this eating plan, you will set him on the road to a healthy diet for life.

IMPLEMENTING THE PLAN

It is not so difficult as it sounds to incorporate five helpings of fresh fruit or vegetables in the daily diet: some fresh or cooked fruit with breakfast, a serving of vegetables and a glass of fruit juice with lunch and a serving of vegetables at supper time, followed by fresh fruit or a fruit pudding makes five helpings (see below).

VEGETABLE REJECTION

Often children raise strong objections to eating vegetables. They may dislike the distinctive taste – the strong flavour of broccoli, for example – or they may find a vegetable's texture off-putting. If you encounter this problem, you could offer fresh fruits, which also provide vitamins, and which can accompany a savoury dish equally well. At other meals, gradually introduce some of the more popular vegetables into your child's diet, such as carrots, sweetcorn and potatoes. Children often prefer vegetables raw to cooked, so you could offer carrot sticks, celery or cucumber pieces. Alternatively, hide vegetables among other ingredients, as in my Pasta Sauce with Hidden Vegetables (see page 72).

FIVE-STAR EATING PLAN

MUESLI WITH FRESH FRUIT FOR BREAKFAST

A MID-MORNING SNACK OF FRESH FRUIT

PASTA WITH BROCCOLI AND CHEESE FOR LUNCH

A DIP WITH VEGETABLE STICKS FOR TEA

CHICKEN SANDWICHES WITH SALAD FOR SUPPER

Making meals fun

Young children, like adults, prefer to eat in company. If your toddler has cutlery he is able to use, is seated at the correct height and has someone to share the meal with, mealtimes will be an enjoyable occasion for him. You may find that he will eat things he has previously rejected, just because a sibling or friend is eating it. Visiting a friend or relative's house often produces the same effect. The excitement of eating in different surroundings, or with other children makes him adventurous enough to try new foods. When you and your child are with other people you may both be more relaxed about the food you are eating. When you are on your own with him, there is a certain amount of unconscious pressure for your child if you are overseeing every mouthful he takes. Consequently, meals can become rather an ordeal. It is easy for both of you to forget that eating should be fun.

EATING SOCIABLY AT HOME

Eating as a family will help your child to integrate into regular mealtimes as well as to learn some of your basic family rules about eating at the table. Even if the whole family can't sit down together at meals during the week – perhaps because the meal is too late for your young child to join in more than occasionally – do sit down beside him while he eats, or ask an older sibling or friend to join him.

A booster seat brings your toddler to the correct table level

COOKING FOR THE FAMILY

By now your toddler should be eating the same meals as the rest of the family. Life is too short to cook a different meal for every member of the family and it is much easier to accustom children to new foods at this early age, when their preferences (and prejudices) are not yet fixed. You can interest him in food, perhaps by talking to him about its form, taste or feel, or by adding a few presentational touches that will appeal to him. However, don't get over-anxious, or angry if he refuses to eat a new dish and don't threaten him with no pudding. Instead, make sure that the pudding on offer is nutritious (see page 78) so that you can relax in the knowledge that he is still eating a healthy diet, even if it's not in the traditional order. Remember that the "balance" of a diet should be assessed over a period of a few days to a week, rather than within a strict limit of 24 hours.

ENCOURAGING SOCIAL SKILLS

Eating with young friends and family makes mealtimes fun and encourages children to eat things they may otherwise turn down.

REMEMBER

◆ YOU CAN NOW introduce cow's milk as your child's usual milk, unless he has special dietary needs.

◆ OFFER PLAIN WATER as a thirst-quencher, or give well-diluted fruit or vegetable juice (using approximately two-thirds water to one-third juice).

◆ IF YOUR BABY has not already learnt to drink from a cup, try to persuade him off a bottle now.

◆ ENCOURAGE YOUR CHILD to eat plenty of fruit and vegetables as part of his meals and as between-meals snacks.

◆ OFFER SIMPLE, easy-to-digest foods after illnesses. Recognize that your child may revert to slightly babyish feeding habits for a short period of time.

When your child is unwell

When children are unwell they often lose their appetite. However, it is important to ensure that your child's fluid intake is maintained. Approximately 80 per cent of a new baby is made up of water (adults are around 70 per cent). Consequently, babies and young children are particularly vulnerable to dehydration during periods of diarrhoea or vomiting. If a child is suffering from either of these problems, stop giving solids and offer plenty of fluids. Special salt and sugar powders that are dissolved in water replace lost minerals and can be bought from pharmacies. Diluted fruit juices,

ice lollipops or flat, caffeine-free soft drinks (take the bubbles out first with ice or a swizzle stick) are suitable for children with diarrhoea. Milk is not suitable.

FOODS DURING ILLNESS

If your child is off his food but not suffering from diarrhoea or vomiting, give liquids that are nutritious – milk, milkshakes (see page 98) or hot chocolate are good. Ice lollipops made from fresh fruit juice, puréed fruit or yogurt are also suitable. Offer simple, easily digested foods, such as homemade chicken soup, steamed fish and mashed potato,

scrambled egg on toast or mashed banana. Antibiotics kill the good bacteria in the body as well as the harmful ones. If your child is taking antibiotics, you could give him live yogurt to help maintain the levels of beneficial bacteria in the body.

CONSTIPATION

If your child is constipated, give him plenty of water and diluted fruit juices. Cut down on sugary and fatty foods and offer fruit, vegetables and wholegrain cereals, but do not overload the digestive system with fibre as this is not a suitable way to relieve constipation in young children. Natural yogurt, prunes and prune juice are more useful in gently relieving it.

REGRESSION

Don't be surprised if your child reverts to more babyish feeding habits even after he has recovered from being ill. While he is ill, he needs extra reassurance in the form of cuddles and he may want his drinks from a bottle again. Until his appetite returns, the memory of his more babyish comforts may make him want to eat the kinds of things you thought he had grown out of. (In fact, this may be the case throughout his early childhood whenever your child is ill.) Try not to worry, he'll soon be back to his old self with a healthy appetite ready to try out new foods again.

DURING ILLNESS
Keep your child's fluid intake high during illness. While he is unwell, he may want to use a bottle or feeding cup that he had previously given up as a kind of comforter.

Food for the Senses

ENCOURAGING YOUR TODDLER to explore the tastes, textures and even the different sounds particular foods make when munched, scrunched and bitten will stimulate his interest in food, and heighten his enjoyment of mealtimes. Even before language skills are very developed, your child will be capable of expressing his responses to new foods, and will enjoy being given plenty of freedom to explore his food with his hands. The foods on these pages are designed to appeal to the eye, to the sense of smell, touch, hearing, and, of course, to the taste-buds.

CHICKEN SAUSAGE SNAILS

A simple dish of chicken sausages and mashed potato becomes, with the help of a little imagination, an eye-catching picture on a plate and an appealing meal. (See page 75 for recipe.)

ROOT VEGETABLE CHIPS

A satisfying crunch is produced by these deep-fried chips of sweet potato, beetroot and parsnip. (See page 70 for recipe.)

TURKEY BALLS & PEPPER SAUCE

Chopped fresh basil perfumes and flavours the delicious sweet pepper sauce that accompanies these juicy miniature meatballs. This dish can be served on a bed of rice but goes equally well with spaghetti. (See page 76 for recipe.)

Show your toddler how to scrunch a sprig of fresh basil in his hands then sniff the bruised leaves

YOGURT PANCAKES
The contrast of sticky maple
syrup, ripe, cool summer fruits
and warm pancakes is appealing.
(See page 78 for recipe.)

RASPBERRY FROZEN YOGURT
Scoops of frosty, frozen yogurt
decorated with chocolate drops
and brittle wafers make a mouth-
watering, and tactile, dessert.
(See page 78 for recipe.)

APRICOT & BLUEBERRY PORRIDGE

350ml (12fl oz) milk

90g (3oz) porridge oats

90g (3oz) ready-to-eat dried apricots, chopped

90g (3oz) blueberries

This makes a simple, nutritious breakfast for your baby. There's no need to blend it for older children.

Pour the milk into a saucepan, bring to the boil and stir in the oats and apricots. Reduce the heat and cook for 3 minutes, stirring. Stir in the blueberries and cook for 2 minutes more. Blend for a few seconds to the desired consistency.

 Preparation/cooking
2 minutes/7 minutes

 Makes 4 portions

 Nutritional information
Rich source of calcium, folate, iron, protein, vitamin A, B vitamins and zinc.

ROOT VEGETABLE CHIPS

1 orange-fleshed sweet potato, scrubbed

1 parsnip, peeled

2 carrots or 1 raw beetroot, peeled

oil for deep frying

freshly ground sea salt

Encourage your child to eat more vegetables by making these crunchy chips. They also make a healthy alternative to packet crisps.

1 Slice all the vegetables wafer thin by hand or by using a slicing blade attachment in a food processor. Heat the oil in a deep-fat fryer or deep pan to 190°C (375°F). Add each vegetable separately, in small batches, and fry until crisp and golden, about 4–5 minutes if using a deep-fat fryer.

2 Remove from the oil and drain on kitchen paper. Sprinkle with sea salt and serve cold.

 Preparation/cooking
10 minutes/15 minutes

 Makes 4 portions

 Nutritional information
Rich source of beta-carotene, fibre, folate and vitamin E.

See page 68 for illustration.

———— TIP ————
You can also make these chips using sliced plantain.

COURGETTE & TOMATO FRITTATA

2 tbsp vegetable oil

1 onion, chopped

175g (6oz) courgettes, thinly sliced

salt and pepper, to taste

2 tomatoes, skinned, deseeded and chopped

4 eggs

1 tbsp milk

2 tbsp freshly grated Parmesan

1 Heat the oil in a 24cm (9½in) non-stick frying pan. Add the onion and courgettes, season lightly and cook for about 15 minutes. Add the tomatoes and continue to cook for 3–4 minutes.

2 Beat the eggs with the milk and pepper, and pour over the vegetables. Cook over a medium heat for about 5 minutes, or until the eggs are set underneath. Preheat the grill to high.

3 Sprinkle the Parmesan over the frittata and cook briefly under the grill until golden (if necessary, wrap the pan handle with foil to prevent burning). Cut into wedges and serve hot or cold.

VARIATIONS

Omit the courgettes and tomatoes. Add 125g (4oz) cooked diced ham and 75g (2½oz) peas to the beaten egg mixture.

Omit the courgettes. Add 1 small diced and sautéed red pepper and 2 cubed boiled potatoes to the egg.

 Preparation/cooking
5 minutes/30 minutes

 Makes 8 portions

 Nutritional information
Rich source of calcium, folate, protein, vitamin A, vitamin B12 and vitamin C.

PASTA CARTWHEELS WITH CHEESE & BROCCOLI

125g (4oz) pasta cartwheels

125g (4oz) broccoli, cut into small florets

60g (2oz) frozen sweetcorn

CHEESE SAUCE

30g (1oz) butter

30g (1oz) flour

300ml (½ pint) milk

pinch of nutmeg

75g (2½oz) grated Cheddar cheese

salt and pepper, to taste

TOPPING

2 tbsp freshly grated Parmesan

1½ tbsp fresh breadcrumbs

1 Bring a pan of lightly salted water to the boil, add the pasta and cook until tender, about 8 minutes, or according to package instructions. Drain and set aside.

2 Meanwhile, place the broccoli and sweetcorn in a steamer and cook for 4–5 minutes, or until tender. Cover to keep warm and set aside.

3 To make the sauce, melt the butter in a small pan. Add the flour to make a paste and stir over a low heat for 1 minute. Gradually whisk in the milk, bring slowly to the boil and cook until thickened, stirring constantly. Remove from the heat, add the nutmeg, stir in the Cheddar until melted, then season.

4 Stir the vegetables into the sauce then mix with the pasta. Pour the mixture into a greased gratin dish, and scatter over the Parmesan and breadcrumbs. Bake in the preheated oven for about 15 minutes.

VARIATION

To make macaroni cheese, omit the vegetables and replace the cartwheels with 150g (5oz) macaroni.

 Preparation/cooking 10 minutes/35 minutes

 Oven temperature 180°C/350°F/gas 4

 Makes 4 portions

 Nutritional information Rich source of calcium, folate, protein, vitamin A, B vitamins and zinc.

 Suitable for freezing Sauce only

PASTA & SAUCE WITH HIDDEN VEGETABLES

2 tbsp olive oil
1 small onion, chopped
1 garlic clove, crushed
75g (2½oz) carrots, chopped
75g (2½oz) courgettes, chopped
75g (2½oz) mushrooms, sliced
400g (13oz) canned chopped tomatoes
125ml (4fl oz) vegetable stock
¼ tsp brown sugar
salt and pepper, to taste
250g (8oz) pasta twists (fusilli)

If your baby is reluctant to eat vegetables, one solution is to resort to disguise. This sauce has lots of vegetables blended into it. Mix it with fun pasta shapes and you are on to a winner! A tablespoon of red pesto makes a nice addition.

1 Warm the oil in a pan, add the onion and garlic, and sauté for about 3 minutes. Add the carrots, courgettes and mushrooms, and cook for about 15 minutes, or until softened. Add the tomatoes, stock and sugar, season to taste, and simmer for 10 minutes. Blend to a purée.

2 Meanwhile, bring a pan of lightly salted water to the boil, add the pasta and cook until tender, about 10 minutes. Toss with the sauce, and serve.

 Preparation/cooking
10 minutes/30 minutes

 Makes 4 portions

 Nutritional information
Rich source of beta-carotene, folate, iron, protein, B vitamins, vitamin C and vitamin E.

 Suitable for freezing
Sauce only

 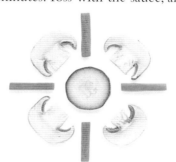 

TUNA & COURGETTE LASAGNE

1 tbsp vegetable oil
1 onion, finely chopped
1 garlic clove, crushed (optional)
2 courgettes, trimmed and sliced
125g (4oz) frozen sweetcorn
400g (13oz) canned chopped tomatoes
250ml (8fl oz) water
2 tbsp tomato purée
300g (10oz) canned tuna
1½ x quantities cheese sauce (see page 71)
9 sheets no pre-cook lasagne
30g (1oz) grated Cheddar cheese, to finish

1 Warm the oil in a frying pan, add the onion and garlic, if using, and sauté until softened. Stir in the courgettes and sweetcorn, and cook for 2 minutes.

2 Add the tomatoes, water and tomato purée. Bring to the boil, then simmer for about 30 minutes. Remove from the heat, add the tuna to the sauce and stir thoroughly. Make the cheese sauce and keep warm.

3 To assemble the lasagne, spoon one third of the tomato and tuna sauce on to the base of a 23 x 15 x 8cm (9 x 6 x 3½in) ovenproof dish. Lay 3 sheets of the lasagne on top, then spoon a third of the warm cheese sauce over the top.

4 Repeat the layering twice, ending with cheese sauce, and sprinkle over the grated Cheddar cheese. Transfer the dish to the preheated oven and cook for about 30 minutes, or until the top is golden and bubbling.

 Preparation/cooking
10 minutes/1 hour 20 minutes

 Oven temperature
190°C/375°F/gas 5

 Makes 8 portions

 Nutritional information
Rich source of calcium, folate, protein, vitamin A, B vitamins, vitamin E and zinc.

 Suitable for freezing

ORZO WITH COLOURFUL DICED VEGETABLES

90g (3oz) soup pasta (orzo)

60g (2oz) carrots, diced

60g (2oz) courgettes, diced

60g (2oz) broccoli, diced

30g (1oz) butter

30g (1oz) freshly grated Cheddar or Parmesan cheese

Orzo is the name given to tiny pasta shapes that resemble barley kernels (you can also find riso or puntalette – "grains of rice"). Its creamy, slightly chewy texture is very appealing to children.

1 Put the pasta in a saucepan together with the diced vegetables, pour over enough boiling water to cover generously and cook for about 12 minutes, or until all the vegetables are tender. Drain thoroughly.

2 Melt the butter in a large pan, stir in the drained pasta and vegetables, then remove from the heat. Add the grated cheese and toss until the cheese has melted.

Preparation/cooking
10 minutes/15 minutes

Makes 4 portions

Nutritional information
Rich source of beta-carotene, folate, protein and vitamin C.

Suitable for freezing

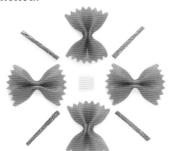
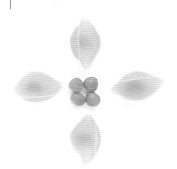

BOW-TIE PASTA WITH HAM & PEAS

150g (5oz) pasta bows (farfalle)

½ vegetable stock-cube

20g (¾oz) butter

15g (½oz) flour

300ml (½ pint) milk

¼ tsp mustard powder

60g (2oz) frozen peas (or a mixture of peas and sweetcorn)

60g (2oz) grated mature Cheddar cheese

60g (2oz) sliced cooked ham, cut into strips

salt and pepper, to taste

Bow-tie pasta is a good shape for young children – don't worry if they treat it as finger food: good manners will come in time! This is also successful made with green and white narrow pasta noodles (tagliolini or taglierini).

1 Bring a pan of water to the boil, add the pasta and stock-cube, and cook until tender, about 10 minutes, or according to package instructions.

2 Meanwhile, make the sauce. Melt the butter in a small pan, stir in the flour to make a paste, then gradually whisk in the milk and mustard. Stir in the peas and cook for 3 minutes. Remove from the heat and stir in the cheese until melted. Add the ham, heat through, season to taste then toss with the pasta.

VARIATION

To make a vegetarian version, omit the ham and add 75g (2½oz) sliced button mushrooms sautéed in a little butter until tender.

Preparation/cooking
5 minutes/15 minutes

Makes 4 portions

Nutritional information
Rich source of calcium, folate, protein, vitamin A, B vitamins and zinc.

Suitable for freezing
Sauce only

JOY'S FISH PIE

250g (8oz) each cod and salmon fillets, skinned

600ml (1 pints) milk

4 peppercorns, 1 bay leaf and a parsley stalk

60g (2oz) butter

1 onion, finely chopped

3 tbsp flour

1 tsp mustard powder

125g (4oz) frozen peas

125g (4oz) sweetcorn

60g (2oz) grated Cheddar

1 tbsp snipped chives

salt and pepper, to taste

MASHED POTATO

750g (1½lb) potatoes, cut into chunks

4 tbsp milk

large knob of butter

salt and pepper, to taste

A good fish pie with creamy mashed potato is one of those ever-popular, old-fashioned nursery foods. This recipe comes from my friend Joy.

1 For the mashed potato, boil some lightly salted water, add the potatoes and boil until tender.

2 Meanwhile, put the fish in a shallow pan with the milk, peppercorns and herbs. Bring to the boil, then cover and cook for 5 minutes, or until the fish flakes easily. Remove the fish, strain the milk and reserve. Flake the fish with a fork and set aside.

3 Melt the butter in a small pan, add the onion and sauté until softened. Stir in the flour to make a paste and cook for 1 minute. Gradually add the strained milk, stirring until the sauce thickens.

4 Mix in the mustard, peas, sweetcorn, chives and most of the Cheddar (keep 2 tbsp to sprinkle over the finished dish). Cook for 4 minutes. Season and add the fish. Put the mixture in a 28 x 18cm (11 x 7in) ovenproof dish.

5 Drain and mash the potatoes. Add milk, butter and seasoning. Spread the potato over the fish, making peaks with a fork. Sprinkle with remaining cheese. Cook in the preheated oven for 25 minutes.

 Preparation/cooking
15 minutes/50 minutes

 Oven temperature
180°C/350°F/gas 4

 Makes 8 portions

 Nutritional information
Rich source of calcium, folate, protein, vitamin A, B vitamins and zinc.

❄ **Suitable for freezing**

——— TIP ———
For an interesting variation, add cooked prawns to the fish and make miniature portions in ramekin dishes.

CREAMY SEAFOOD WITH RICE

175g (6oz) basmati rice, rinsed

125g (4oz) each cod and salmon fillets, skinned

300ml (½ pint) milk

3 peppercorns, 1 bay leaf and a parsley stalk

30g (1oz) butter

1 small onion, finely chopped

2 tbsp flour

30g (1oz) frozen peas

90g (3oz) cooked prawns

30g (1oz) grated Cheddar cheese

salt and pepper, to taste

1 tomato, skinned, deseeded and chopped

1 Bring a pan of lightly salted water to the boil. Add the rice and cook until tender, about 11 minutes.

2 Meanwhile, put the cod and salmon fillets in a shallow pan with the milk, peppercorns and herbs. Bring to the boil, then cover and simmer for 5 minutes, or until the fish is cooked and flakes easily. Remove the fish with a slotted spoon, strain the milk and reserve. Cut the fish into chunks.

3 Warm the butter in a small pan, add the onion and sauté until just softened. Stir in the flour to make a paste and cook for 1 minute. Gradually add the strained milk, stirring until the sauce thickens.

4 Add the fish to the sauce with the frozen peas and prawns, and heat through. Remove from the heat, stir in the grated cheese and season to taste. Arrange a portion of fish on a bed of rice and sprinkle over some chopped tomato.

 Preparation/cooking
10 minutes/20 minutes

 Makes 4 portions

 Nutritional information
Rich source of folate, protein, B vitamins, incl. B12, and zinc.

 Suitable for freezing

——— TIP ———
This creamy sauce would also make a good sauce for pasta shells (conchiglie).

Make a slightly larger version of this dish for an older child

CHICKEN SAUSAGE SNAILS

CHICKEN SAUSAGES

375g (12oz) raw, skinned boneless chicken breast, cubed

1 small onion, finely chopped

½ tbsp chopped fresh parsley

½ chicken stock-cube, finely crumbled

1 small apple, peeled and grated

2 tbsp fresh breadcrumbs

salt and pepper, to taste

flour for coating

vegetable oil for frying

MASHED POTATO

500g (1lb) potatoes, cut into chunks

1 tbsp milk

15g (½oz) butter

salt and pepper, to taste

TO DECORATE

shredded savoy cabbage

1 carrot, cut into sticks

16 frozen peas

tomato ketchup

Using a little imagination you can make succulent homemade chicken sausages into a fun and visually appealing meal.

1 Put the chicken in a food processor with the onion, parsley, crumbled stock-cube, apple and breadcrumbs. Chop for a few seconds then season the mixture lightly.

2 Form the mixture into 4 sausages each about 12cm (5in) long. Spread the flour on a plate and use to coat the sausages. Heat the vegetable oil in a frying pan, add the sausages and sauté for about 15 minutes, turning occasionally, or until browned on all sides and cooked through.

3 Meanwhile, place the potatoes in the bottom of a steamer, cover with lightly salted water and cook until tender. Five minutes before the potatoes are done, put the vegetables for decorating in the top of the steamer and cook until tender. Mash the potatoes with the milk, butter and seasoning.

4 To assemble, form the potato into 4 dome shapes using an ice-cream scoop and decorate with a ketchup spiral to create a snail-shell effect (you can use a piping bag with a small nozzle for this, or cut a small hole in the corner of a freezer bag and use that). Put a sausage underneath each dome of potato. Use the steamed carrot sticks and peas to make the snail's feelers, and arrange the cabbage as grass.

 Preparation/cooking
20 minutes/1 hour 10 minutes

 Makes 4 portions

 Nutritional information
Rich source of folate, protein, B vitamins and zinc.

 Suitable for freezing
Chicken sausages only

TURKEY BALLS & PEPPER SAUCE

TURKEY MEATBALLS

500g (1lb) minced turkey

1 onion, finely chopped

1 small apple, peeled and grated

3 tbsp fresh breadcrumbs

1 egg, lightly beaten

2 tbsp chopped fresh sage
or thyme

salt and pepper, to taste

flour for coating

2 tbsp vegetable oil for frying

RED PEPPER SAUCE

1½ tbsp vegetable oil

2 shallots, finely chopped

1½ red peppers, deseeded
and chopped

1 tsp tomato purée

3 tbsp chopped fresh basil

450ml (¾ pint) vegetable stock

salt and pepper, to taste

*Served with rice or spaghetti, these little meatballs
make a great lunch. If you have time, roast
and skin the peppers for the sauce, which can also
be made with chicken stock (see page 46).*

1 To make the red pepper sauce, heat the oil in a
frying pan, add the shallots and red peppers, and
sauté until softened. Stir in the remaining ingredients
and season to taste. Bring to the boil and simmer
for 15–20 minutes. Blend until smooth.

2 Mix together all the ingredients for the
meatballs, seasoning to taste. Use your hands to
form the mixture into about 24 walnut-sized balls.
Spread the flour on a plate and use to coat the
meatballs. Heat the oil in a frying pan, add the balls
and sauté until golden all over.

3 Transfer the meatballs to a casserole, cover with
pepper sauce, and cook in the preheated oven
for about 20 minutes, or until the meatballs are
cooked through and well browned.

 Preparation/cooking
20 minutes/40 minutes

 Oven temperature
180°C/350°F/gas 4

 Makes 8 portions

 Nutritional information
Rich source of beta-carotene,
folate, iron, protein, B
vitamins and zinc.

 Suitable for freezing

TIP

These can be made ahead and
frozen, then simply defrosted
and re-heated in a microwave
(just make sure you test the
temperature before giving them
to your child).

FINGER PICKING CHICKEN & POTATO BALLS

125g (4oz) potatoes, chopped

125g (4oz) parsnips, chopped

3 tbsp vegetable oil

½ small onion, finely chopped

1 carrot, grated

125g (4oz) boneless chicken breast, cut into chunks

large knob of butter

flour for coating

Mashed potato and parsnip give these balls a soft texture and a hint of sweetness, and they are just the right size for picking up and nibbling.

1 Put the potatoes and parsnips in a pan, cover with water, bring to the boil then simmer, covered, for 12–15 minutes, or until tender.

2 Meanwhile, heat 1 tablespoon of oil in a frying pan, add the onion and carrot, and sauté for 4–5 minutes. Add the chicken and continue to sauté for about 10 minutes, or until cooked through.

3 Drain the potatoes and parsnips and mash with half the butter until smooth. Finely chop the chicken, onion and carrot in a food processor and mix with the mashed vegetables.

4 Form the mixture into about 24 walnut-sized balls. Spread the flour on a plate and use to coat them. Heat the remaining oil and butter in a frying pan, add the meatballs and sauté until golden.

 Preparation/cooking
10 minutes/40 minutes

 Makes 8 portions

 Nutritional information
Rich source of beta-carotene, folate and protein.

Suitable for freezing

SHEPHERD'S PIE

1½ tbsp vegetable oil

1 large onion, chopped

1 small red pepper, finely chopped

1 garlic clove, crushed

500g (1lb) lean minced lamb

300ml (½ pint) chicken stock (see page 46) or beef stock

1 tbsp chopped fresh parsley

½ tsp yeast extract

1 tbsp tomato purée

¼ tsp Worcestershire sauce

175g (6oz) mushrooms, sliced

MASHED POTATO

2lb (1kg) potatoes, roughly chopped

45g (1½oz) butter

3 tbsp milk

salt and pepper, to taste

1 Warm the oil in a pan, add the onion, red pepper and garlic, and sauté until softened. Add the meat and sauté until browned. If desired, transfer the cooked mixture to a food processor and chop for a few seconds on the pulse setting.

2 Transfer the meat to a saucepan and add the stock, parsley, yeast extract, tomato purée, Worcestershire sauce and mushrooms. Cook over a medium heat for about 20 minutes.

3 Meanwhile, boil the potatoes in lightly salted water until tender, then drain and mash with 30g (1oz) of butter and the milk. Season to taste.

4 Arrange the meat either in one large dish or in individual ramekins, cover with the mashed potato and dot the topping with the remaining butter. Cook in the preheated oven for 20 minutes.

VARIATION

To make cottage pie, replace the minced lamb with the same quantity of lean minced beef. For the topping, omit the mashed potato and replace it with 2lb (1kg) mashed swede, or use a combination of mashed swede and potato.

 Preparation/cooking
15 minutes/1 hour 10 minutes

 Oven temperature
180°C/350°F/gas 4

 Makes 8 portions

 Nutritional information
Rich source of folate, iron, protein, vitamin A, B vitamins and zinc.

 Suitable for freezing

—— TIPS ——
To make minced meat more palatable to young children, cook it first and then chop it in a food processor.

If preferred, make the shepherd's pie in individual ramekins and decorate with vegetable faces (see page 103).

RASPBERRY FROZEN YOGURT

250g (8oz) frozen or fresh raspberries

4 tbsp caster sugar

125ml (4fl oz) water

300–350ml (½ pint–12fl oz) mild natural yogurt

6 tbsp crème fraîche

2–3 tbsp icing sugar

This can also be made with a mixture of berries – perhaps strawberries, blackberries and raspberries. A few minutes before you want to eat it, take it from the freezer and allow to soften slightly. Serve by itself or with some fresh raspberries.

1 Put the raspberries in a saucepan with the sugar and water. Bring to a simmer, then cook for 5 minutes. Purée using a hand blender, then strain through a sieve to get rid of the seeds. Leave to cool.

2 Stir the yogurt and crème fraîche into the raspberry purée and add enough icing sugar to sweeten. Transfer to an ice-cream maker and freeze for about 20 minutes.

VARIATION

Mix 375ml (13fl oz) cherry yogurt with 6 tablespoons of crème fraîche. Stir in 200g (7oz) canned stoned black cherries, 100ml (3½fl oz) maple syrup and 45g (1½oz) grated plain chocolate. Transfer to an ice-cream maker, and freeze as described above.

Preparation/cooking
2 minutes/35 minutes, incl. 20 minutes freezing

Makes 8 portions

Nutritional information
Rich source of calcium, folate, protein, vitamin B2, vitamin C and vitamin B12.

See page 69 for main illustration.

— TIP —
If you don't have an ice-cream maker, put the mixture in a plastic tub. Freeze for 1 hour then remove and beat by hand or in a food processor to break up the ice crystals. Freeze again, repeating the beating procedure once or twice during freezing.

YOGURT PANCAKES

1 egg, lightly beaten

150ml (¼ pint) mild full-fat natural yogurt

150ml (¼ pint) milk

100g (3½oz) self-raising flour

¼ tsp salt, or 2 tbsp maple syrup (for a sweeter version)

vegetable oil for frying

TO ACCOMPANY

pure maple syrup

fresh fruit, such as strawberries, raspberries or sliced peaches

These mini pancakes are delicious served with fresh fruit and maple syrup. You could also add a few sultanas to a maple syrup-sweetened batter to make sultana pancakes.

1 Mix together the beaten egg and the yogurt, then stir in the milk, flour, and salt or maple syrup. Mix until you have a smooth batter.

2 Heat a little oil in a frying pan until sizzling hot. Drop heaped tablespoons of batter into the pan, leaving plenty of space around each one, and flatten slightly with a palette knife. They should spread to about 6cm (2½in) across. Cook for 1–2 minutes until lightly browned, then turn and cook for a further 1–2 minutes until browned on the other side and set in the centre.

3 Drizzle the pancakes with maple syrup and serve scattered with fruit.

Preparation/cooking
2 minutes/10 minutes

Makes 8 portions

Nutritional information
Rich source of calcium, folate, protein, vitamin B2 and vitamin B12 (served with fruit).

Suitable for freezing
See tip below

See page 69 for illustration.

— TIP —
These pancakes can be layered between pieces of waxed or greaseproof paper and then frozen. They can be reheated in a toaster.

BANANA CHIPS WITH HONEY YOGURT DIP

4 bananas, cut lengthways into thin strips

icing sugar mixed with a sprinkling of cinnamon (optional)

natural yogurt sweetened with honey

These fruit chips can also be made with mango. You could serve them with a fruity fromage frais dip.

1 Place the strips of banana on a baking sheet lined with greased baking parchment or waxed paper. Bake for about 1 hour in the preheated oven.

2 Remove from the oven, leave to cool then peel the chips off the paper. Dust with icing sugar and cinnamon, if liked, and serve with the yogurt.

   Preparation/cooking
2 minutes/1 hour

 Oven temperature
110°C/225°F/gas low

 Makes 8 portions

 Nutritional information
Rich source of vitamin C.

JELLY BOATS

2 large oranges, halved

1 x 135g (4½oz) packet fruit jelly, e.g. strawberry or orange

1 small can mandarin orange segments (optional)

1 small punnet fresh raspberries (optional)

TO DECORATE

8 small rice paper triangles

8 party cocktail sticks

Of all the foods I make for parties, these ingeniously simple jellies are perhaps the most popular.

1 Squeeze the juice from the oranges (keep it to make into a drink) without breaking the skin. Carefully scrape out the membrane and discard.

2 Make the jelly according to packet instructions, reducing the amount of water specified by a quarter if using fruit. Divide the fruit, if using, between the orange halves then fill with jelly and refrigerate until set.

3 Take a wet knife and cut each orange half in half again. Thread a cocktail stick down the centre of each rice paper triangle, then set the sail in the jelly.

VARIATION

To make shaped jellies, make the jelly according to packet instructions, using half the amount of water specified on the packet. Pour into a deep non-stick baking tray and refrigerate until set. Cut into shapes using a wet knife (see page 105 for illustration).

Preparation/cooking
5 minutes/10 minutes, plus 1¾ hours setting

Makes 8 portions

NOTE

These jelly boats use cocktail sticks. For young children, place the boats on each child's plate then remove the cocktail sticks before they begin to eat.

 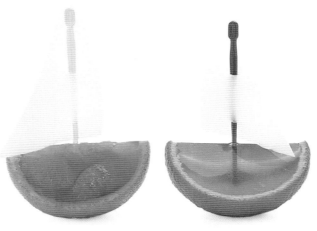 

18 Months – 2 Years

FOOD TASTES ARE DECIDED EARLY IN LIFE, SO YOU SHOULD
AIM TO ESTABLISH A VARIED, HEALTHY DIET FOR YOUR
CHILD WHILE SHE IS STILL RECEPTIVE TO NEW FOODS.
HOWEVER, DESPITE YOUR BEST EFFORTS, YOUR PLANS MAY
BE DERAILED BY A PERIOD OF FADDY OR ERRATIC EATING,
AND YOU MAY HAVE TO USE A LITTLE INGENUITY TO
STIMULATE HER APPETITE. THIS CHAPTER IS FULL OF IDEAS
FOR HEALTHY "FAST FOODS" THAT SHOULD ENCOURAGE
EVEN THE MOST RELUCTANT CHILD TO TRY NEW FOODS.

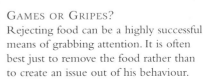

The Active Toddler

TODDLERHOOD IS A TIME of growing individuality. Your child will have attained a much higher level of physical coordination and she will be displaying her personality and temperament both verbally and physically. As your toddler works to establish her character, she may begin to exert an independent spirit at mealtimes; this may call for consistent but sensitive treatment.

Busy bodies

As your child nears her second birthday, her growth rate slows down substantially. At the same time, her levels of activity are on the increase because she has greater physical competence and probably a busier, more active daily schedule. Consequently, your rounded baby will become a slimmed-down, active toddler,

losing much of her "puppy fat". Although she has high energy requirements, her small stomach will probably cope best with light meals interspersed with "top-up" snacks. Remember that toddlers are not conditioned into eating by the clock, and, quite sensibly, will tend to want to eat only when they are truly hungry. By

this age they will be fairly vocal in their preferences and you will want to give your child easily prepared food that you can rustle up quickly before her hungry demands become furious outbursts (see pages 86-87). Of course you will want to create some structure and routine for family mealtimes, but keep flexible. The last thing you want to do is make an issue over "correct" mealtimes, turning your child into a resentful eater.

TANTRUMS

Remember that your child is entering the stage of toddler tantrums when the frustrations she encounters can lead her to explode with rage. It is hard for you too, and you may need to try out a number of ways to encourage her eating (see page 85). Avoid using bribes to get her to eat, however, as you will only encourage difficult behaviour.

GAMES OR GRIPES?
Rejecting food can be a highly successful means of grabbing attention. It is often best just to remove the food rather than to create an issue out of his behaviour.

Snacks

Colourful and easy-to-handle snacks have wide appeal. An occasional treat of chocolate or crisps will do no harm, but these foods offer only "empty" calories that provide instant but short-lived energy and shouldn't replace healthy snacks. Carbohydrate should be your child's main energy source. Starches, as found in pasta, wholemeal bread and cereals are excellent energizing foods as they release calories slowly and help to keep energy levels at a constant. For healthy snacks try:

◆ Chunky tomato & cream cheese dip (see page 88)
◆ Shaped sandwiches (see page 89)
◆ Pasta salad (see page 108)

PASTA SALAD
WITH VEGETABLE PIECES

WHOLEMEAL
SANDWICHES

CREAMY DIP
WITH VEGETABLES

"GRAZING" HABITS

It is easy to misjudge exactly how much your child is eating, particularly if your family tends to snack rather than sit down for meals. If you are worried that your child's food intake is low, and that the amounts of food she consumes at mealtimes are frequently miniscule, try to keep a diary of her total food intake over a period of a few days, perhaps a week. Many children have the habit of "grazing" – taking a little food here and there. However, if all these snacks are added up over the period you have monitored, you may find that your child's diet is reasonably substantial and balanced.

Limiting sugary foods

As toddlers are exposed to an increasingly varied diet, they may be quick to acquire a "sweet tooth". Since they are most likely to pick up their eating habits from the immediate family, you may need to be strong-minded yourself if you want your child to have a low sugar intake. It is not just the amount of sugar we eat that harms our teeth but also the frequency with which we put sugary foods in our mouth: each time we eat sugary foods, the bacteria in dental plaque produce acids that attack tooth enamel and can cause tooth decay. Consequently, a packet of sweets consumed all in one go does less harm than eating the sweets over a prolonged period of time. It is also much better to confine sugary foods to mealtimes because eating other foods at the same time dilutes the acid and reduces the harmful effects of the sugar. Moreover, at mealtimes there is more saliva in the mouth to wash away acids. Cheese is particularly beneficial at the end of a meal as it helps to reduce acid saliva.

SWEETS AS A REWARD

Do not let sweets and puddings become synonymous with rewards: try to offer other treats, such as stickers or comics. Consider making a rule that sweets are allowed only at certain times, even once a week, perhaps on Sundays.

SWEET DRINKS

Even pure fruit juices contain fructose (a natural sugar) which can cause tooth decay, so confine diluted fruit juices to mealtimes, where they can also benefit your child by increasing the absorption of iron from food. Read labels carefully; sugar can be disguised under other names such as glucose, maltose or dextrose. Some individual cartons of fruit juice contain as much as 30g (1oz) of sugar. Diet soft drinks are no kinder to teeth as they too contain acids that attack tooth enamel. Sweet drinks at bedtime are not a good idea, since saliva won't wash away the acid during the night and you'll destroy any good work done by toothpaste.

The fussy eater

Refusing food is one of the first ways young children can flex their muscles and assert their drive for independence. It doesn't take them long to realize how easy it is to manipulate you at the dinner table. Indeed, battles at mealtimes are often one of the most stressful aspects of early parenthood. Cajoling a child to eat – whether in the form of bribery, threats, even the frantic production of a culinary masterpiece – is usually counter-productive.

KEEPING CALM

However unreasonable your child's eating habits seem to be, try to respond calmly. The aim is to help your child slot into normal family eating, not to force her into co-operation. Don't put pressure on your child to eat the foods you want her to eat. Aim to keep the emotional temperature down: food shouldn't be used as a means to teach a child to do as she is told. It is an unfortunate fact of life that many children seem to enjoy stretching their parents' patience to the limit: after all, refusing to eat makes them the centre of attention. The only way to counter this aspect of the problem is to refuse to be riled; simply take the rejected meal away. Attempting to induce guilt also won't work: don't make a child feel that she has a moral duty to leave a clean plate – it is unlikely to motivate a 2-year-old into finishing her dinner. It helps

to remember that no young child ever starves herself and that her fussy diet may well be nutritious, if unconventional. Rather than worry about your child's diet on a daily basis, remember that it is the balance of her diet over several days that really matters.

FADDY EATING

Occasionally children go through periods of eating only a few specific foods. If, for example, your child wants only peanut butter sandwiches at every meal, don't worry too much. Make sure the bread is wholemeal and maybe slip in some sliced banana or give her a milkshake or a glass of milk to accompany the sandwich, and continue to offer some tasty and nutritious alternatives. Children can thrive on quite a limited range of foods and, except in rare cases, will eventually get bored of a monotonous diet. Sometimes fads may be more pronounced, and appear even more irrational: your child might refuse foods that have come into contact with each other on her plate, for instance, so a sectioned plate may provide a solution to this temporary phase.

REJECTING SPECIFIC FOODS

If your child continually rejects a particular food, you can assume that she really doesn't like it. Sometimes it is best to respect your child's wishes: after all, adults have likes and dislikes. Try to recognize when your child is

USING CUTLERY
By 18 months your child may have the dexterity to use a spoon and fork. Letting her have her own cutlery and plate may make her a more enthusiastic eater.

being stubborn and when she has a genuine dislike of a particular food. If vegetables are a problem, there are many ways to disguise them in the diet (see page 65). Meat is another food that is often rejected. A healthy diet need not include meat provided your child's diet includes milk and dairy products, beans and pulses or soya-based products, which will provide adequate quantities of protein, iron and B vitamins (see page 37). However, it is often the texture rather than the taste of meat that children object to. Your child may dislike lumps of meat, but dishes such as spaghetti bolognese (see page 61) or shepherd's pie (see page 77) may make meat more palatable, particularly if the meat is blended until fairly smooth. You could also make bite-sized meatballs (see page 97) and serve them with ketchup, or mince meat very finely, moisten with gravy and mix it into a combination of mashed potato and carrot.

More strategies

You may have to try several ways of encouraging your child to eat well. Aim to respond creatively to some of her behavioural quirks, but don't cast all rules aside. Try to be the one who takes the initiative, rather than being ruled by your child: consistency is also important.

ALLOWING INDEPENDENCE

Give your child scope to assert her independence, perhaps by letting her choose two out of three vegetables offered to her. You can also involve her in food preparation or let her choose fruit when you go shopping. It is sensible to keep portions small and give second helpings if requested. Your child will then feel that she has control over how much she eats, and won't be put off by a heaped plate.

SNACKING
Offer a few easily managed finger foods that can be eaten at leisure.

MAKE MEALTIMES SOCIABLE

Mealtimes are social occasions, so set a good example by eating with your child as often as possible, then encourage her to eat what you are enjoying (and avoid distractions like television). Inviting a friend to tea, adding a few appealing presentational touches, or changing the venue can work wonders.

CHANGING THE VENUE
A teddy bear's picnic outdoors will make tea-time into a great treat.

Fast Foods for Toddlers

THE ACTIVE TODDLER'S HUNGER rarely coincides with
regular mealtimes. Because she uses up energy so quickly
with her new-found independence, light, frequent snacks
may best suit her needs. She is also too young to wait patiently for meals,
so it is a good idea to be able to offer easy-to-prepare, healthy "fast foods".
All the foods shown here are visually appealing and have interesting
textures and vibrant flavours – and all can be eaten on the run.

*Cherry tomato
and tofu kebabs
(see page 92)*

*Carrot stars made
with a miniature
biscuit cutter*

KEBABS IN PITTA POCKETS
Miniature kebabs can be grilled, taken
off the skewers and stuffed into warm
pitta bread pockets with some colourful
salad leaves. Chicken with tomatoes,
and tofu with chunky vegetables are
delicious combinations. (See pages
92 and 96 for recipes.)

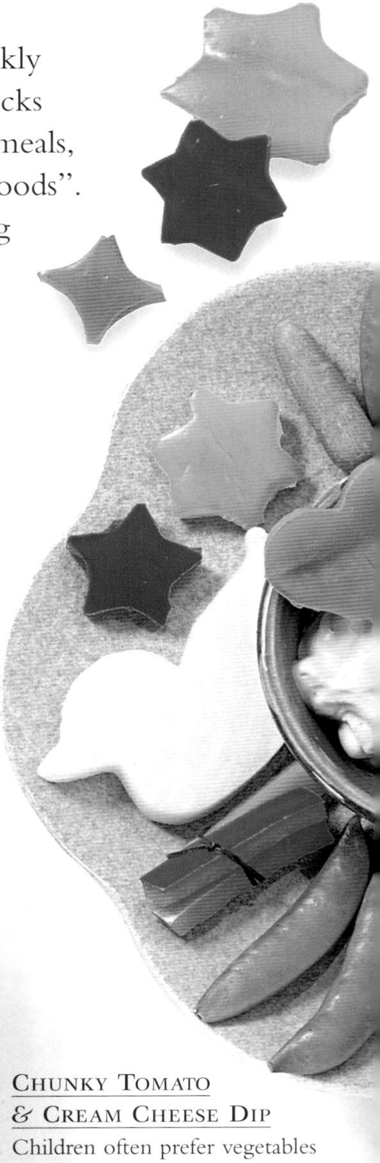

CHUNKY TOMATO
& CREAM CHEESE DIP
Children often prefer vegetables
raw, especially if cut into whimsical
shapes, and they love dunking
them into dips. This makes a
nutritious between-meals snack.
(See page 88 for recipe.)

PINWHEEL SANDWICHES
Toddlers will adore
these sticky spirals of soft
brown bread rolled with
their favourite fillings.
(See page 89 for recipe.)

*Kebabs with
honey and
citrus marinade
(see page 89)*

MINI PIZZAS

Brown and white muffins
simply split in half, spread
with a good tomato sauce,
cheese and plenty of
different toppings make
excellent pizzas. Animal–
face patterns will be
especially popular.
(See page 91 for recipe.)

*Amusing
animal faces
are simple
to create*

*Cheese and salad
double-deckers*

*Cheese and
chive kite*

SHAPED
SANDWICHES

The most versatile
of fast foods, shaped
sandwiches make savoury
mouthfuls. (See page 89 for recipes.)

SCRAMBLED EGGS WITH CHEESE & TOMATO

2 eggs

1 tbsp milk or single cream

salt and pepper, to taste

15g (½oz) butter

1 tomato, skinned, deseeded and chopped

2 tbsp grated Gruyère cheese

Scrambled eggs make a quick and nutritious family breakfast. Serve them with a toasted bagel or buttered toast. For a special breakfast or brunch, add strips of smoked salmon.

1 Beat the eggs with the milk and season lightly. Melt the butter in a saucepan over a low heat, add the chopped tomato and sauté for 1 minute.

2 Add the egg mixture and heat, stirring continuously with a wooden spoon, until the eggs start to cook. Add the cheese and continue to stir until the eggs are set. Serve immediately.

Preparation/cooking
2 minutes/6 minutes

Makes 2 portions

Nutritional information
Rich source of calcium, iron, protein, vitamin A, B vitamins and vitamin E.

APPLE, MANGO & APRICOT MUESLI

45g (1½oz) each chopped dried mango and apricots

30g (1oz) sultanas or raisins

125g (4oz) muesli base, or 60g (2oz) each of oat and wheat flakes

30g (1oz) finely chopped hazelnuts (optional)

350ml (12fl oz) apple and mango juice or plain apple juice

½ red apple, cored and chopped

extra fresh fruit, such as banana or raspberries (optional)

Unfortunately many breakfast cereals designed for children are low in nutrients and high in sugar. I make a healthy, Swiss-style muesli for my family using a bought muesli base – a mixture of rolled oats, wheat, barley and rye flakes – and fresh fruit. This mix, without the added fresh fruit, can be kept refrigerated for several days.

Soak the dried fruit, muesli base and nuts in the juice overnight or for several hours. In the morning stir in the apple and your chosen extra fresh fruit.

VARIATION

Make a deliciously unusual muesli by substituting grape juice for the apple juice and using chopped dried peaches instead of mango and apricots.

Preparation
5 minutes, plus overnight soaking

Makes 4 portions

Nutritional information
Rich source of fibre, folate, iron, protein, vitamin A, B vitamins and zinc.

— NOTE —
This recipe contains nuts. Avoid if there is a family history of nut allergy.

CHUNKY TOMATO & CREAM CHEESE DIP

200g (7oz) soft cream cheese

3 tbsp mayonnaise

1 tbsp tomato ketchup

1 tsp fresh lemon juice

¼ tsp Worcestershire sauce

¼ tsp soy sauce

½ tbsp snipped chives

2 tomatoes, skinned, deseeded and chopped

Serve this appealing dip with raw and cooked vegetables, bread soldiers or pitta toasts for a tasty and energizing snack.

Simply mix all the ingredients together, blending them thoroughly, and spoon into small bowls.

VARIATION

To make a cream cheese and chive dip, mix together the same quantities of soft cream cheese and mayonnaise with 3 tablespoons of milk. Mix in 1 teaspoon of Dijon mustard, 2 tablespoons of snipped chives, a pinch of sugar and freshly ground pepper to taste.

Preparation
10 minutes

Makes 8 portions

Nutritional information
Rich source of vitamin A, vitamin B12 and vitamin E.

See page 86 for illustration.

— TIP —
This dip can also be made with low-fat dairy produce, but only for older children.

SHAPED SANDWICHES

Sandwiches make a quick snack that can be eaten on the run; what's more you can use all sorts of fillings and types of bread. Those that use foods from each of the main groups — bread, fruit and vegetables, meat and alternatives, dairy products — are a nutritious alternative to cooked meals.

EGG MAYONNAISE
CUT-OUT DUCKLING

CUCUMBER AND CHEESE
OPEN SANDWICH

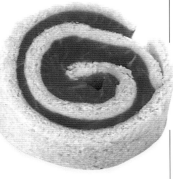

EGG MAYONNAISE AND
AVOCADO DOUBLE-DECKER

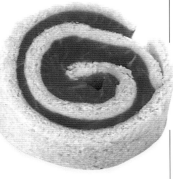

SMOKED SALMON PINWHEEL

OPEN SANDWICHES

Cut slices of bread into simple shapes, or into animal shapes using biscuit cutters. Butter and then spread with filling. Try cottage cheese or mashed egg sheep or ducks; geometric shapes spread with a favourite filling, such as diamond-shaped bread kites spread with mashed avocado, or with thinly sliced ham, turkey or chicken; or bread and cheese squares decorated to look like parcels with red pepper or chive ribbons. (See pages 87 and 104 for additional illustrations.)

DOUBLE-DECKER SANDWICHES

Take 3 slices of buttered brown or white bread, with the centre slice buttered on both sides. Sandwich together with 2 complementary but contrasting fillings, such as sliced banana and strawberry jam; grated cheese, shredded lettuce and yeast extract; or mashed avocado and egg mayonnaise. Cut into strips. (See page 87 for additional illustrations.)

PINWHEEL SANDWICHES

Trim the crusts off 2 thin slices of bread. Overlap the edges slightly and flatten with a rolling pin so that they join together. Butter and spread with a colourful filling and roll up, Swiss-roll-fashion. Cut across into thin rounds. Suggested fillings: peanut butter and jam, cream cheese and mashed avocado, egg mayonnaise with cress. (See page 87 for additional illustrations.)

MINI PITTA BREAD POCKETS

Warm a small pitta bread, cut in half and fill with a savoury mix, for example grated cheese or shredded chicken or ham with salad; sliced hard-boiled egg with lettuce; or mashed sardines and sliced tomato.

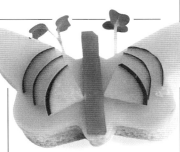

SALAD AND CHEESE
CUT-OUT BUTTERFLY

CHEESE AND RED PEPPER
OPEN SANDWICH

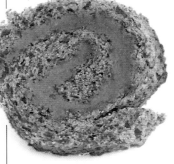

WHOLEMEAL PINWHEEL
WITH SPINACH PÂTÉ

PITTA BREAD POCKET

89

ALPHABET PASTA MINESTRONE

2 tbsp vegetable oil

1 onion, finely chopped

125g (4oz) carrots, diced

½ celery stalk, finely chopped

30g (1oz) leeks, white part only, finely chopped

125g (4oz) potatoes, chopped

60g (2oz) courgettes, diced

2 ripe tomatoes, skinned, deseeded and chopped

1.5 litres (2½ pints) chicken stock (see page 46)

2 tsp tomato purée

60g (2oz) frozen peas

45g (1½oz) alphabet pasta

salt and pepper, to taste

Homemade minestrone makes a nutritious soup for children, and also becomes a satisfying family meal if supplemented by bread and salad. You can add shredded cabbage (about 125g/4oz) to make it even more substantial, if you like. The tiny alphabet pasta shapes appeal to children.

1 Heat the oil in a large pan, add the onion and sauté for about 5 minutes. Add the carrots, celery and leeks, and sauté until they begin to soften, about 5 minutes. Add the potatoes and courgettes and sauté for 2–3 minutes.

2 Stir in the chopped tomatoes, stock and tomato purée. Bring to the boil, then cover and simmer for 20 minutes. Add the frozen peas, return the soup to the boil, and cook for 5 minutes.

3 Stir in the alphabet pasta, return the soup to the boil, then simmer for about 5 minutes. Taste and season lightly.

    Preparation/cooking
10 minutes/45 minutes

Makes 8 portions

Nutritional information
Rich source of beta–carotene, fibre, folate, vitamin A and vitamin C.

Suitable for freezing

— TIP —
This soup can also be made with vegetable stock.

BOW-TIE PASTA WITH SPRING VEGETABLES

125g (4oz) pasta bows (farfalle)

30g (1oz) butter

30g (1oz) leeks, finely chopped

60g (2oz) carrots, diced

60g (2oz) courgettes, diced

60g (2oz) broccoli, cut into very small florets

salt and pepper, to taste

150ml (¼ pint) single cream

30g (1oz) freshly grated Parmesan

This is simple to prepare but never fails to please. You can use other pasta shapes, such as tagliatelle or penne, with the creamy sauce.

1 Bring a pan of lightly salted water to the boil, add the pasta and cook until tender, about 10 minutes, or according to package instructions.

2 Meanwhile, melt the butter in a heavy-based saucepan, add the leeks and carrots, and sauté for about 5 minutes. Add the diced courgettes and broccoli and cook for about 7 minutes, or until all the vegetables are tender. Season to taste.

3 Pour in the cream and cook, stirring, for 1 minute. Remove from the heat and stir in the Parmesan. Toss the pasta with the sauce, and serve.

    Preparation/cooking
10 minutes/20 minutes

Makes 4 portions

Nutritional information
Rich source of beta–carotene, calcium, fibre, folate, protein, vitamin B12, vitamin C and zinc.

Suitable for freezing
Sauce only

Use mushroom slices, uncooked cheese and black olives for the eyes and nose

Sweetcorn kernel teeth

DECORATED MINI PIZZAS
Quirkily decorated small pizzas have instant child appeal. Older children can make their own toppings using a selection of prepared ingredients.

MOUSE FACE PIZZA
Use steamed courgette pieces for ears, stuffed olive slices for eyes, a black olive for the nose, and strips of carrot for whiskers.

MINI PIZZAS

Adding a selection of colourful vegetables to mini pizzas is a great way to encourage your child to eat more vegetables. For a special occasion, you might like to make animal face designs as shown above.

2 muffins, split in half, or 1 small baguette, cut in half

4 tbsp good tomato sauce (homemade or bought)

60g (2oz) grated Cheddar, Gruyère or mozzarella cheese

ADDITIONAL TOPPING

15g (½oz) butter

1 tbsp chopped spring onion

60g (2oz) courgettes, thinly sliced

60g (2oz) mushrooms, sliced

salt and pepper, to taste

sweetcorn kernels, raw pepper strips, cheese shapes, olives and fresh basil leaves (optional)

1 To make the topping, warm the butter in a pan, add the spring onion and sauté for 1 minute. Add the courgettes and mushrooms, and sauté until just tender, about 4 minutes. Season to taste.

2 Lightly toast the muffins or baguette. Divide the tomato sauce between each of the cut sides of muffin or baguette, spread evenly, then scatter with cheese. Top with cooked vegetables, perhaps making patterns or animal faces, then cook under a preheated grill until the cheese is bubbling and golden. If desired, use the sweetcorn, uncooked pepper and cheese, olives and basil to decorate further.

Preparation/cooking
10 minutes/15 minutes

Makes 4 portions

Nutritional information
Rich source of calcium, protein, vitamin A and B vitamins.

See page 87 for additional illustration.

SWEETCORN, CHERRY TOMATO & TOFU KEBABS

275g (9oz) firm tofu, cubed

6 baby sweetcorn, halved

1 courgette, trimmed and sliced into round chunks

8 cherry tomatoes

4 mini pittas, split in half

salad leaves, to garnish

MARINADE

1½ tbsp soy sauce

1½ tbsp runny honey

1½ tbsp Chinese plum sauce

1 tbsp vegetable oil

1 spring onion, finely chopped

Tofu (soya bean curd) is a nutritious alternative to meat. Although naturally bland, it is delicious marinated as it soaks up flavours well, and its soft texture appeals to children.

1 Combine the ingredients for the marinade in a small jug. Put the tofu in a shallow bowl and pour over the marinade. Cover and leave to soak for about 1 hour. While the tofu marinates, soak 4 wooden skewers in cold water.

2 Thread alternate pieces of tofu, sweetcorn, courgette and the tomatoes on the skewers. Brush with some of the marinade. Cook under a hot grill or on the barbecue for about 3 minutes on each side, basting occasionally, or until the vegetables are tender and the tofu is nicely browned.

3 Slide the kebabs off the skewers, arrange in the pitta pockets and garnish with salad leaves.

Preparation/cooking
1 hour 5 minutes, incl.
1 hour marinating/
6 minutes

Makes 4 portions

Nutritional information
Rich source of calcium, fibre, folate, iron, protein, vitamin A, vitamin C, vitamin E and zinc.

See page 86 for main illustration.

TIP
The sweetcorn and courgette may be parboiled before skewering, if preferred.

MULTI-COLOURED RICE WITH KIDNEY BEANS

1 tbsp olive oil

½ onion, chopped

1 garlic clove, crushed

30g (1oz) each red and green pepper, deseeded and chopped

30g (1oz) carrots, diced

125g (4oz) long-grain white rice, rinsed

300ml (½ pint) chicken stock (see page 46) or vegetable stock

1 tomato, skinned, deseeded and chopped

45g (1½oz) frozen peas

60g (2oz) cooked red kidney beans

Combining kidney beans with rice creates a high quality protein for children who don't like eating meat. The bright colours look very appealing.

1 Warm the oil in a pan. Add the onion and garlic, and sauté until softened. Add the peppers and carrots, and sauté for 2 minutes, stirring occasionally. Stir in the rice and cook for 2–3 minutes.

2 Pour in the chicken stock, add the chopped tomato and bring the mixture to the boil. Reduce the heat, cover and simmer for 10 minutes.

3 Remove the cover, add the peas and beans, and cook, stirring occasionally, for 6 minutes or until the rice and vegetables are tender.

VARIATION
Omit the kidney beans and add 75g (2½oz) each diced ham and canned or frozen sweetcorn.

Preparation/cooking
5 minutes/25 minutes

Makes 4 portions

Nutritional information
Rich source of beta-carotene, fibre, folate, protein, vitamin C and zinc.

SWEET & SOUR VEGETABLE STIR-FRY

1½ tbsp vegetable oil

1 onion, cut into rings

60g (2oz) baby sweetcorn, cut into quarters

60g (2oz) carrots, sliced thinly and cut into shapes with a tiny biscuit cutter

90g (3oz) broccoli, cut into small florets

90g (3oz) beansprouts

30g (1oz) red pepper, cored, deseeded and cut into strips

1 spring onion, finely chopped

pinch of black pepper

SWEET & SOUR SAUCE

150ml (¼ pint) vegetable stock

½ tbsp cornflour blended with 1 tbsp cold water

2 tsp soft brown sugar

½ tbsp soy sauce

One of the most appealing ways to encourage your child to eat vegetables is to make a colourful stir-fry. It's important to ensure that the vegetables remain crisp to retain their flavour and nutrients.

1 Heat the oil in a wok or frying pan. Add the onion and sauté until softened, about 5 minutes. Add the sweetcorn, carrots and broccoli, and stir-fry for 2 minutes.

2 Add the beansprouts, red pepper and spring onion, and stir-fry for a further 2 minutes. Season with a little black pepper.

3 To make the sauce, blend the vegetable stock with the cornflour paste in a small pan. Mix in the brown sugar and soy sauce. Set over a high heat, bring to the boil and simmer for about 2 minutes, until the sauce is thickened. Toss the hot vegetables with the sauce, and heat through in the wok.

Preparation/cooking
15 minutes/15 minutes

Makes 4 portions

Nutritional information
Rich source of beta-carotene, fibre, folate, iron and vitamin C.

—— TIP——
For young children, blanch the carrots and broccoli first to make them softer to chew.

VEGETARIAN CROQUETTES

500g (1lb) potatoes, peeled and roughly chopped

knob of butter

salt and pepper, to taste

75g (2½oz) broccoli, cut into small florets

75g (2½oz) carrots, chopped

45g (1½oz) frozen sweetcorn

60g (2oz) Cheddar cheese

60g (2oz) ready salted crisps, crushed

1 Bring a large pan of lightly salted water to the boil, add the potatoes and cook until tender. Drain and mash with the butter and seasoning.

2 Meanwhile, place the vegetables in a steamer and cook until tender, 6–7 minutes. Mix into the mashed potato and season to taste.

3 Cut the cheese into 8 sticks. Use your hands to shape the potato and vegetable mixture around the cheese to form 8 sausage-shaped croquettes.

4 Roll the croquettes in the crushed crisps until well coated and place on a baking tray. Transfer to the preheated oven and bake for 15 minutes.

 Preparation/cooking
10 minutes/40 minutes

 Oven temperature
180°C/350°F/gas 4

 Makes 8 portions

 Nutritional information
Rich source of beta-carotene, calcium, fibre, folate, protein, vitamin B12 and vitamin C.

 Suitable for freezing

ANNABEL'S VEGETABLE RISSOLES

200g (7oz) sweet potato, peeled

100g (3½oz) butternut squash or pumpkin, peeled

150g (5oz) potato

75g (2½oz) leeks, white part only, finely chopped

150g (5oz) mushrooms, chopped

2 tbsp chopped fresh parsley

125g (4oz) breadcrumbs

½ tbsp soy sauce

½ lightly beaten egg

salt and pepper, to taste

flour for coating

vegetable oil for frying

These are good eaten hot or cold and would be ideal for a lunch box or picnic.

1 Grate the sweet potato, squash and potato. Using your hands, squeeze out some of the excess moisture from the grated pulp.

2 In a mixing bowl, combine all the vegetables with the parsley, breadcrumbs, soy sauce and beaten egg. Season to taste.

3 Form the mixture into about 12 walnut-sized rissoles. Spread the flour on a plate and use to coat the rissoles lightly.

4 Heat the oil in a large frying pan, add the rissoles and sauté over a medium heat for 8–10 minutes, turning occasionally, until golden on the outside and cooked through.

 Preparation/cooking
25 minutes/10 minutes

 Oven temperature
180°C/350°F/gas 4

 Makes 4 portions

 Nutritional information
Rich source of beta-carotene, calcium, fibre, iron, B vitamins, vitamin C and vitamin E.

 Suitable for freezing

TIP
This recipe is best made with soft white breadcrumbs, but you can use wholemeal breadcrumbs

SALMON STARFISH

500g (1lb) cold mashed potatoes

2 tbsp tomato ketchup

1 tsp Worcestershire sauce

1 egg, lightly beaten

2 tbsp chopped chives

375g (12oz) cooked salmon fillets, flaked

3 tbsp fresh breadcrumbs, plus extra for coating

a little melted butter

I serve these with shredded runner bean "seaweed" and Special Tomato Sauce (see page 122).

1 Mash the potatoes with the tomato ketchup, Worcestershire sauce, egg and chives. Mix in the salmon and 3 tablespoons of breadcrumbs. Shape the mixture into flat rissoles.

2 Use a large star-shaped biscuit cutter to cut 8 starfish shapes. Gently pull out the points of the stars. Coat with breadcrumbs and brush with butter.

3 Set the fishcakes on a lightly greased baking sheet. Transfer to the preheated oven and cook for 4 minutes on each side.

 Preparation/cooking
20 minutes/8 minutes

 Oven temperature
180°C/350°F/gas 4

 Makes 8 portions

 Nutritional information
Rich source of folate, protein, B vitamins and vitamin D.

 Suitable for freezing

—— TIP ——
These fishcakes can be shallow-fried instead of oven-baked.

MINI GOLDEN FISH BALLS

vegetable oil for shallow frying

knob of butter

1 onion, finely chopped

500g (1lb) minced or finely chopped fish, such as haddock, bream, whiting, cod or hake

60g (2oz) carrots, finely grated

1 tbsp chopped fresh parsley

2 dessertspoons caster sugar

½ lightly beaten egg

1 tbsp flour

salt and pepper, to taste

These are just the right size for toddlers to pick up. They are not at all fishy and have an appealing, slightly sweet taste. My fishmonger prepares a mixture of minced fish, but you could make your own mixture in a food processor.

1 Heat a tablespoon of vegetable oil and the butter in a small frying pan. Add the onion and sauté for about 5 minutes, or until just softened.

2 Put the minced fish in a mixing bowl and stir in the onion, carrots, parsley, sugar, beaten egg and flour. Season to taste then form the mixture into about 24 balls about the size of a large cherry tomato.

3 Heat a further 3 tablespoons of vegetable oil in the frying pan. Add the fish balls and fry for about 10 minutes, until golden brown all over. Drain on kitchen paper.

 Preparation/cooking
5 minutes/20 minutes

 Makes 8 portions

 Nutritional information
Rich source of protein, vitamin A, vitamin B12 and vitamin E.

 Suitable for freezing

ONE-POT RICE WITH CHICKEN

2 tbsp olive oil

1 onion, finely chopped

60g (2oz) carrots, diced

1 tbsp chopped fresh parsley

125g (4oz) chicken breast, diced

175g (6oz) basmati rice, rinsed

350ml (12fl oz) chicken stock
(see page 46)

200g (7oz) canned chopped
tomatoes

60g (2oz) frozen peas

2 tbsp freshly grated Parmesan

Unlike a real risotto which needs a lot of attention, this rice dish is easy to make. You can omit the chicken and add extra vegetables.

1 Warm the oil in a pan. Add the onion and sauté until softened. Add the carrots and parsley and sauté for 2–3 minutes. Add the chicken and cook for 2–3 minutes.

2 Add the rice to the pan and stir for 1 minute. Pour in the chicken stock and stir in the tomatoes and peas. Bring the mixture to the boil, then cover and simmer for 15 minutes.

3 Remove the cover and cook, stirring occasionally, for 5 minutes, or until the rice is tender. Remove from the heat and stir in the Parmesan.

 Preparation/cooking
5 minutes/30 minutes

 Makes 8 portions

 Nutritional information
Rich source of beta-carotene, calcium, folate, protein and zinc.

 Suitable for freezing

CRUNCHY CHICKEN FINGERS

salt and pepper, to taste

30g (1oz) flour

1 chicken breast, cut
into 6 strips

1 small egg, lightly beaten

45g (1½oz) cornflakes,
crushed with a rolling pin

2 tbsp vegetable oil

These crunchy chicken pieces make a tasty finger food. Serve them with a little bowl of ketchup.

1 Lightly season the flour and put into a plastic bag. Add the chicken pieces and shake until coated.

2 Dip the chicken fingers in beaten egg then roll them in the cornflakes. Heat the oil in a frying pan, add the chicken and sauté for about 6 minutes on each side, or until crunchy on the outside and cooked through.

 Preparation/cooking
5 minutes/13 minutes

 Makes 2 portions

 Nutritional information
Rich source of folate, iron, protein and B vitamins.

 Suitable for freezing
Before cooking

CHICKEN KEBABS WITH HONEY & CITRUS MARINADE

1 boneless chicken breast and
4 thighs, skinned and trimmed

½ red pepper, cut into chunks

½ small onion, cut into chunks

4 mini pittas, split in half

salad leaves, to garnish

MARINADE

1 tbsp soy sauce

1 tbsp runny honey

1 tbsp each freshly squeezed
lemon juice and orange juice

1 tsp vegetable oil

Use your own choice of vegetables for these tasty kebabs, perhaps mushrooms or courgettes.

1 Combine the marinade ingredients in a bowl. Cut the chicken into small chunks and add to the marinade with the pepper and onion. Cover and leave for at least 30 minutes. While the chicken marinates, soak 4 wooden skewers in cold water.

2 Thread alternate pieces of chicken, pepper and onion on to the skewers. Transfer to a hot grill or barbecue and cook for about 5 minutes on each side, or until cooked through and nicely browned.

3 Slide the kebabs off the skewers, arrange alternate pieces of chicken and vegetable in the pitta bread pockets and garnish with salad leaves.

 Preparation/cooking
35 minutes/10 minutes

 Makes 4 portions

 Nutritional information
Rich source of beta-carotene, folate, iron, protein, B vitamins, vitamin C and zinc.

See page 86 for illustration.

——— TIP ———
Add ½ tablespoon of sesame seeds to the marinade for extra flavour, if liked.

CHICKEN BOLOGNESE

2 tbsp vegetable oil

1 shallot, finely chopped

1 garlic clove, crushed

1 leek, trimmed and sliced

500g (1lb) minced chicken

1 carrot, diced

400g (13oz) canned chopped tomatoes

125ml (4fl oz) water

1 tsp caster sugar

2 tsp tomato ketchup

2 tsp fresh thyme leaves

salt and pepper, to taste

You can use minced chicken or turkey to make a delicious pasta sauce. This version would make a good cannelloni filling. If you don't have fresh thyme, substitute ½ teaspoon of dried thyme.

1 Warm the vegetable oil in a frying pan, add the shallot and garlic, and sauté over a low heat for 2–3 minutes. Add the leek and sauté for about 3 minutes, until beginning to soften.

2 Add the chicken, breaking it up with a fork so that it does not stick together, and sauté for about 3 minutes. Add the carrot and then stir in the remaining ingredients.

3 Bring the mixture to the boil and then simmer for about 20 minutes, stirring occasionally, until the vegetables are tender and the chicken is cooked through. Season lightly and serve with pasta.

Preparation/cooking
5 minutes/30 minutes

Makes 8 portions

Nutritional information
Rich source of beta-carotene, folate, protein, B vitamins and zinc.

Suitable for freezing

LAMB MEATBALLS WITH A SWEET & SOUR SAUCE

MEATBALLS

250g (8oz) minced lamb

1 onion, finely chopped

½ red pepper, finely chopped

1 tbsp finely chopped fresh parsley

1 small apple, peeled and grated

salt and pepper, to taste

flour for coating

2 tbsp vegetable oil for frying

SWEET & SOUR SAUCE

400g (13oz) canned chopped tomatoes

1 tbsp malt vinegar

1 tbsp brown sugar

1 tbsp tomato ketchup

dash of Worcestershire sauce

These light and succulent meatballs in a tangy tomato-based sauce are delicious served with rice or pasta. They also make a good finger food served plain.

1 Mix together all the ingredients for the meatballs, seasoning to taste, then form the mixture into about 16 small balls. Spread the flour on a plate and use to coat the meatballs on all sides.

2 Heat the vegetable oil in a frying pan, then add the meatballs and sauté for 10–15 minutes, turning them occasionally, until browned and almost cooked through.

3 Meanwhile, mix together all the ingredients for the sauce in a small pan set over a medium–high heat and cook for 4 minutes. Taste and season if necessary.

4 Pour the sauce over the meatballs in the frying pan and cook over a medium heat for about 10 minutes, or until the sauce has thickened and the meatballs are cooked through.

Preparation/cooking
20 minutes/25 minutes

Makes 8 portions

Nutritional information
Rich source of folate, iron, protein, B vitamins, incl. B12, and zinc.

Suitable for freezing

RAISIN & OATMEAL BISCUITS

100g (3½oz) unsalted butter

90g (3oz) granulated sugar

90g (3oz) light brown sugar

1 egg

1 tsp vanilla extract

125g (4oz) plain flour

1 tsp mixed spice

½ tsp baking powder

½ tsp bicarbonate of soda

¼ tsp salt

75g (2½oz) porridge oats

175g (6oz) raisins

1 Cream together the butter and sugars in an electric mixer, or by hand. Beat in the egg and vanilla extract.

2 Sift together the flour, mixed spice, baking powder, bicarbonate of soda and salt. Add to the mixture and beat until just combined. Stir in the oats and raisins.

3 Lightly grease 2 baking sheets. Using your hands, form the dough into about 22 walnut-sized balls. Put them on the baking sheets, widely spaced, and flatten them down a little.

4 Transfer the biscuits to the preheated oven and bake for about 10 minutes, or until lightly golden all over. Transfer to a wire rack and leave to cool. Store in an airtight container.

 Preparation/cooking
20 minutes/10 minutes

 Oven temperature
190°C/375°F/gas 5

 Makes 22 biscuits

 Suitable for freezing

BANANA MUFFINS

60g (2oz) bran flakes

300ml (½ pint) milk

125g (4oz) wholemeal flour

½ tsp salt

1 tbsp baking powder

60g (2oz) butter

60g (2oz) caster sugar

1 egg

2 bananas, mashed

90g (3oz) raisins

These muffins are full of good natural ingredients. They make superb portable food and can be eaten on the run if there's no time for a proper breakfast.

1 Soak the bran flakes in the milk for 10 minutes. Sift together the flour, salt and baking powder.

2 Cream together the butter and sugar then beat in the egg. Stir in alternate spoonfuls of soaked bran flakes and flour mixture. Gently fold in the mashed bananas and the raisins.

3 Line a muffin tray with paper cases and half-fill each case with mixture. Bake in the preheated oven for 30 minutes.

 Preparation/cooking
15 minutes/30 minutes

 Oven temperature
180°C/350°F/gas 4

 Makes 12 muffins

 Nutritional information
Rich source of fibre, folate, iron and B vitamins, incl. B12.

 Suitable for freezing

STRAWBERRY & BANANA SMOOTHIE

125g (4oz) strawberries

1 small banana, cut into chunks

140g (4½oz) vanilla yogurt

4 tbsp milk, plus extra as necessary

Fruit and yogurt smoothies make tasty and nutritious drinks. For a special treat, substitute vanilla ice-cream for the yogurt.

Process all the ingredients with a hand-held blender until smooth. Add extra milk to thin if necessary.

VARIATION

Mix 2 tablespoons of hot milk with 3 tablespoons of instant malt powder. Add 150ml (¼ pint) cold milk, 2 scoops of chocolate ice-cream and 2 broken-up chocolate cookies (optional). Blend until smooth.

 Preparation
5 minutes

 Makes 2 portions

 Nutritional information
Rich source of calcium, folate, protein, vitamin B12 and vitamin C.

— TIP —
If the strawberries are not very sweet, you can add a little sugar or honey.

THREE-TIER
ICE LOLLIPOP

SUMMER FRUITS
ICE LOLLIPOP

ORANGE, PINEAPPLE
AND PASSIONFRUIT
ICE LOLLIPOP

HOMEMADE ICE LOLLIPOPS

250g (8 z) fresh or frozen summe fruits (such as strawber es, raspberries, blueberries, itted cherries, blackberries and redcurrants)

2 tbsp icing sugar, sieved

150ml (¼ pint) low-sugar blackcurrant fruit drink

300g (10oz) raspberry or strawberry yogurt

500ml (17fl oz) freshly squeezed fruit juice, such as tropical crush with mixed fruit juices

There is one food that children are almost guaranteed to like – ice lollipops. These lollipops are made with ingredients that are actually good for your child: puréed fruits, yogurt and fresh fruit juices. The three-tier version looks very attractive, but you can make up a single fruit flavour using the juice of your choice.

1 Put the summer fruits in a pan with the sugar and cook over a low heat for a few minutes, until soft and mushy. Purée in a blender, stir in the blackcurrant drink then strain through a sieve. Set aside to cool.

2 Pour the mixture into 10–12 lollipop moulds, filling them about a third full, and freeze. When the first layer is set, pour in yogurt to a depth of 2.5cm (1in) and freeze. Once this layer is frozen, pour in the fresh juice almost to the top, and place the cover with its stick over each lollipop. Freeze again.

3 When ready to eat, run the mould under the hot tap for a few seconds to loosen the lollipops.

VARIATION

Put a strawberry slice into each of 12 moulds. Mix 900ml (1½ pints) strained freshly squeezed orange juice with 350ml (12fl oz) pineapple juice or exotic fruit juice. Add the strained juice of 6 passionfruit. Pour into the moulds, cover and freeze.

 Preparation
3–4 hours, incl. freezing time

 Makes 12 lollipops
(or 10 if using larger moulds)

 Nutritional information
Rich source of vitamin C.

—— TIP ——
Adding a slice of fruit or a fresh raspberry before pouring in the juice can look very attractive.

2-3
Years

By the time your child reaches his second birthday, he should be joining regularly in family meals and continuing to broaden his tastes. This is an excellent time to encourage an active interest in food, perhaps by allowing him to participate in fun, simple cooking tasks, or to help choose favourite dishes for a birthday tea with friends.

Early Childhood

CHILDREN IN THIS AGE GROUP are often highly appreciative of their food, especially when it has the lively presentation of a party spread. It is surprising just how quiet a group of 2 to 3 year-olds can be around a table laden with edible goodies. Others are more erratic and selective. Whatever his eating habits, your child will spend a lot of time with you in the kitchen and will enjoy joining in with your cooking activities.

Eating for an active day

Two and three-year-olds are highly active and often appear, if not thin, at least leggy. Your child will still need frequent small meals to meet his high energy requirements and there may be times when he seems in need of a rapid energy "fix" to stop him becoming over-tired or grumpy.

Sugar and carbohydrates from refined sources (such as fizzy drinks or chocolate biscuits) are quickly broken down into glucose and provide an instant "pick-me-up", but fruit or fruit juice are healthier energy sources that are also fast-working. Unrefined carbohydrate foods, such as bread, potatoes or homemade biscuits (see page 98) take longer to break down into glucose, but provide a more sustained energy supply.

"TOP UP" FOODS

FOR A QUICK SPURT OF ENERGY:
- Bowl of cornflakes
- Pieces of fruit, fresh or dried
- Yogurt with honey

FOR A STEADY STREAM OF ENERGY:
- Raw vegetables with dips
- Bread with ham, tuna or cheese
- Jacket potato with filling
- Baked beans on toast
- Salad with hard-boiled egg
- Oatcakes or rice cakes with cheese
- Freshly made fruit milkshakes

Cooking: a new activity

You can encourage your child's interest in food by involving him in its preparation early on. Children often take great pride in helping to lay the table, knead dough or mix ingredients, and can be fascinated by quite ordinary tasks that adults take for granted: just think how many ways there are to prepare an egg, or how ingredients change shape, texture and colour if heated or frozen. All this is a new experience for your child. Provided you keep him away from sharp knives or electrical equipment, there are plenty of supervised activities he can take part in, from breaking eggs into a bowl to cutting out biscuits with shaped cutters. There are simple recipes in this book that would be ideal for your child to help you make. Try Mini Pizzas (page 91), Cheesy Bread Animals (page 106), Character Fairy Cakes (page 114), Shortbread Cookies (page 115) or Chewy Apricot & Cereal Bars (page 130).

LEARNING NEW SKILLS Some of the messiest activities will be the most enjoyable. Let your child feel free to experiment.

Making mealtimes work

By the age of 2 your child will be able to sit on a secured booster seat at table with you, and he will be eating very much what the rest of the family eats, though perhaps at different times. It is important, however, to keep him company at mealtimes if he is having his supper before the rest of the family. Leaving him sitting alone at the table, even if you are in the same room, is bound to lead to trouble as he fights for your attention. Aim to encourage his enjoyment of food: try to include him in the family's lunch or evening meal as often as possible. Don't feel obliged to make novelty foods all the time, but do think about giving everyday meals some quick "child appeal". Without spending more than a few moments, a simple plate of food can be made to appeal to a child's sense of form and colour; fresh fruit arranged in a pattern on his plate will bring a smile to his face and stimulate his interest.

"MOCK FRIED EGG"
Vanilla yogurt with half an apricot on top becomes a simple visual joke.

SAVOURY DIP
A colourful array of vegetable and bread sticks has instant appeal.

SHEPHERD'S PIE
Make a mini portion in a ramekin and let your child decorate it as he wishes.

REMEMBER

♦ STOCK SUPPLIES of simple to prepare but nutritious foods that will sustain your child's energy levels.

♦ DON'T MAKE YOUR CHILD wait too long for a meal once he has announced that he is hungry: he is not yet capable of waiting patiently and will probably become irritable.

♦ ENCOURAGE A TASTE for foods that are not high in sugar while your child is still young. If sugar is kept to a minimum now, he is much less likely to develop a sweet tooth later.

♦ IF YOUR CHILD becomes somewhat territorial about his "special" cutlery and crockery, humour his whim.

♦ INVOLVE YOUR CHILD in simple food preparation to encourage his interest in food and enjoyment of meals.

OBESITY

The most common nutritional disorder in the western world is obesity. Research suggests that childhood obesity may be related to adult obesity and that this association becomes stronger as childhood progresses. Obesity is a problem that tends to run in families, though a hereditary link has not been proved. However, by adopting a long-term approach to healthy eating, it should be possible to ensure that your child's weight keeps apace of his increasing height. If a child is already obviously overweight, most medical experts would encourage parents to adopt a healthier eating pattern as a family, rather than cut down on the amount of food offered. No child should ever go hungry, but if 99 per cent of the diet consists of carbohydrates from starchy and cereal sources, fruit and vegetables, low-fat dairy foods and fish or lean meat, then sugary, fatty and processed foods are edged out and become a minimal part of the diet. Most babies do go through a chubby stage, especially before they learn to walk, and this is perfectly natural and healthy. Chubbiness tends to disappear as children become more active; indeed improved levels of physical activity are a key factor in controlling obesity. Even a walk to the shops or a game of catch in the park will help use up energy, improve muscle tone and build strong bones. A purely slimming diet should not be an option for growing children.

Party Time

HERE ARE PARTY DISHES that taste and look wonderful. You can plan the party tea around a theme, perhaps serving foods with different distinctive shapes, as here, or choosing a colour scheme. Don't provide only sweet foods: the healthier savoury dishes can be made to look just as appealing, but do serve them before you bring out the sweet things.

OPEN SANDWICHES

Daintily cut open sandwiches make easy finger foods for small children. These sandwiches are spread with butter or cream cheese, then topped with rounds of cucumber or tomato, squares of mild cheese or ham, or rosettes of smoked turkey. (See page 89 for recipe.)

ANNABEL'S PASTA SALAD

A dish of multi-coloured pasta with plenty of vegetable chunks and a lively dressing should appeal to both small children and any accompanying parents. (See page 108 for recipe.)

Use biscuit cutters to shape these nuggets

SHORTBREAD COOKIES & SHAPED JELLIES

These iced biscuits can be made well ahead, and in any shape. The jelly shapes in the centre continue the star theme. (See pages 115 and 79 for recipes.)

A flower design is made with balls of icing

PARCEL CAKE

A bold and bright birthday sponge cake shaped to look like an array of parcels makes a superb centrepiece. (See page 115 for recipe.)

HEART-SHAPED CHICKEN NUGGETS

These chicken and apple patties, with their moist interior and crunchy coating, will be an instant hit with children. (See page 110 for recipe.)

TOMATO SOUP

1 tbsp olive oil

1 garlic clove, crushed

1 onion, chopped

75g (2½oz) carrots, diced

400g (13oz) canned chopped tomatoes or 8 fresh tomatoes

1 tbsp tomato purée

600ml (1 pint) vegetable stock

2 slices white bread, shredded

salt and pepper, to taste

pinch of sugar

2 tbsp torn fresh basil leaves

A really good homemade tomato soup is usually a great favourite with children. I prefer to use canned tomatoes as so many fresh tomatoes lack flavour, but if you have ripe, full-flavoured, medium-sized tomatoes, you can use them instead.

1 Warm the olive oil in a large pan over a low heat, then add the garlic, onion and carrots, and sauté for 10 minutes, stirring occasionally.

2 Add the remaining ingredients except for the basil. Simmer for 10 minutes, stirring occasionally, until all the vegetables are soft.

3 Stir in the basil and simmer for a further 5 minutes. Liquidize using a blender.

Preparation/cooking
10 minutes/26 minutes

Makes 8 portions

Nutritional information
Rich source of beta-carotene and folate.

Suitable for freezing

CHEESY BREAD ANIMALS

250g (8oz) strong plain flour, plus flour to dust

pinch of salt

½ sachet (½ tbsp) fast action dried yeast

½ tsp honey

pinch of cayenne pepper

1 tsp mustard powder

approximately 150ml (¼ pint) warm water

60g (2oz) grated mature Cheddar cheese

2 tbsp freshly grated Parmesan

TO DECORATE

1 egg, beaten

currants

sesame seeds

poppy seeds

grated Cheddar cheese

Children adore making bread – it's a bit like playing with playdough – and they will have great fun forming this delicious cheesy bread into animal shapes.

1 Sift the flour and salt into a mixing bowl. Stir in the yeast, honey, cayenne pepper and mustard and just enough of the water to form a soft dough.

2 Transfer to a floured surface and knead lightly for about 5 minutes to make a smooth, pliable dough. Gradually knead the grated cheeses into the dough (this will produce a slightly streaky effect).

3 Shape the dough into 6 animal figures and transfer to a floured baking sheet. Cover them loosely with a tea-towel and leave to rise in a warm place for about 1 hour, or until doubled in size.

4 Brush with beaten egg and add currants for eyes. Sprinkle the tops with sesame seeds, poppy seeds or grated cheese. Transfer to the preheated oven and bake for 20 minutes, or until golden brown. The underside should sound hollow when tapped. Leave on a wire rack to cool.

VARIATION

To make cheese and onion bread rolls, add 1 tablespoon of finely chopped spring onion to the dough at the end of step 2.

Preparation/cooking
1½ hours, incl. 1 hour rising/20 minutes

Oven temperature
200°C/400°F/gas 6

Makes 6 bread rolls

Nutritional information
Rich source of calcium, folate, protein, vitamin B12 and zinc.

Suitable for freezing

TUNA &
SWEETCORN
FILLING

CRANBERRY &
TURKEY FILLING

BARBECUE
BEAN FILLING

MINI BAKED POTATOES

3 small baking potatoes

oil and sea salt, for brushing

CRANBERRY & TURKEY FILLING

1 tsp cranberry sauce

1 tbsp smooth peanut butter

1 tsp milk

60g (2oz) shredded turkey

TUNA & SWEETCORN FILLING

60g (2oz) cooked sweetcorn

2 tbsp mayonnaise

60g (2oz) flaked tuna, drained

1 spring onion, finely sliced

freshly ground black pepper

1 tbsp grated Cheddar cheese

BARBECUE BEAN FILLING

250g (8oz) canned barbecue baked beans, or 250g (8oz) plain baked beans seasoned with Worcestershire sauce

1 tbsp grated Cheddar cheese

Small baked potatoes look especially attractive when made into little sailing ships decorated with a cheese triangle sail and a red pepper flag. Each of the fillings suggested here is sufficient for 3 potatoes.

1 Wash the potatoes, pat dry, prick with a fork, brush with oil and sprinkle with a little sea salt. Place in the preheated oven and bake for about 40 minutes, or until crispy on the outside and tender inside (test with a skewer).

2 Cut the potatoes in half, scoop out the flesh into a bowl and mash thoroughly. Mix the ingredients from your chosen topping with the mashed potato then spoon the mixture back into the skins. If using grated cheese, sprinkle a little over each of the potatoes.

3 Place the potatoes under a preheated grill (they can be arranged in a muffin tray to keep them upright). Heat for a few minutes, or just until lightly golden on top. If desired, decorate the potatoes as boats, securing the cheese sails with cocktail sticks.

 Preparation/cooking
10 minutes/45 minutes

 Oven temperature
200°C/400°F/gas 6

 Makes 6 portions

 Nutritional information
Rich source of folate, protein and vitamin B12. (For Cranberry & Turkey Filling)
Rich source of folate, protein and vitamin B12. (For Tuna & Sweetcorn Filling)
Rich source of folate, fibre and protein.(For Barbecue Bean Filling)

❄ **Suitable for freezing**
Undecorated only

—— NOTE ——
If decorating as sailing boats, remove the cocktail sticks as soon as your child is served.

THOUSAND ISLAND SALAD DRESSING

6 tbsp natural yogurt

3 tbsp mayonnaise

3 tbsp tomato ketchup

½ tsp Worcestershire sauce

salt and pepper, to taste

This versatile dressing goes well with a green salad, or sliced tomatoes and avocado. You could add 1 tablespoon of finely chopped parsley to garnish.

Simply blend all the ingredients together, transfer to a clean container and refrigerate, or whisk thoroughly and use immediately.

 Preparation
2 minutes

 Makes 4 portions

 Nutritional information
Rich source of vitamin B12 and vitamin E.

ANNABEL'S PASTA SALAD

150g (5oz) pasta bows (farfalle)

60g (2oz) French beans

60g (2oz) carrots, sliced

100g (3½oz) frozen sweetcorn

4 cherry tomatoes, quartered

DRESSING

30g (1oz) onion, grated

4 tbsp vegetable oil

1 tbsp white wine vinegar

2 tbsp water

½ tsp chopped fresh ginger root

1 tbsp chopped celery

1 tbsp soy sauce

1½ tsp tomato purée

1 tsp caster sugar

salt and pepper, to taste

This salad's delicious dressing is popular with my children as a dip for raw vegetables (I make up a big bottle of it to keep in the fridge). The salad is great for lunch boxes, picnics or as a side dish served warm or cold. Use three-colour pasta if possible.

1 Bring a pan of lightly salted water to the boil, add the pasta and cook until tender, about 10 minutes, or according to package instructions.

2 Meanwhile, put the beans and carrots in a steamer and cook for 4 minutes. Add the sweetcorn to the steamer and cook for 3–4 minutes, or until tender.

3 Combine all the ingredients for the dressing in a blender or food processor, adding only a little salt and pepper, and process until smooth. Combine the cooked pasta with the vegetables and cherry tomatoes and toss with some of the dressing.

VARIATION

Add 30g (1oz) diced cucumber, 75g (2½oz) diced cold chicken or tuna to this salad, and vary the vegetables, according to taste.

 Preparation/cooking
10 minutes/12 minutes

 Makes 4 portions

 Nutritional information
Rich source of beta-carotene, fibre and folate.

See page 104 for main illustration.

PENNE WITH SWEETCORN, TUNA & TOMATO

200g (7oz) canned tuna in oil (preferably yellowfin tuna)

1 garlic clove, crushed

1 small onion, sliced

175g (6oz) pasta quills (penne)

400g (13oz) canned chopped tomatoes

1 tbsp tomato purée

2 tbsp chopped fresh parsley

125g (4oz) frozen sweetcorn

salt and pepper, to taste

30g (1oz) freshly grated Parmesan

This is a simple, popular pasta dish that can be rustled up using mainly store cupboard ingredients. I like to make this using light-meat (yellowfin) tuna.

1 Drain the oil from the tuna into a frying pan and set it over a low heat. Add the garlic and onion, and sauté until softened.

2 Meanwhile, bring a pan of lightly salted water to the boil, add the pasta and cook until tender, about 9 minutes, or according to package instructions.

3 Add the tomatoes, tomato purée and parsley to the frying pan, and cook for 10 minutes. Add the sweetcorn and let the sauce simmer for 5 minutes. Flake the tuna into a bowl, then mix with the sauce and season lightly.

4 Drain the pasta and toss it with the sauce. Spoon into an ovenproof dish, sprinkle with Parmesan and set under a preheated grill for 2–3 minutes, until bubbling and golden.

 Preparation/cooking
5 minutes/25 minutes

 Makes 4 portions

 Nutritional information
Rich source of calcium, fibre, iron, protein, B vitamins, incl. B12, and zinc.

—— Pasta with Courgettes, Peppers & Sausages ——

1 tbsp vegetable oil

1 small onion, sliced

60g (2oz) red peppers, cut into diamond shapes

100g (3½oz) courgettes, sliced

300ml (½ pint) passata

½ chicken stock-cube, finely crumbled

125g (4oz) pasta bows (farfalle)

100g (3½oz) sausages, cooked and sliced

1 Warm the oil in a frying pan, add the onion and sauté until softened. Add the peppers and cook for 3–4 minutes. Add the courgettes and cook for 3 minutes more.

2 Pour the passata into the pan then stir in the crumbled stock-cube. Bring the mixture to the boil, then cover and simmer for 10 minutes.

3 Meanwhile, bring a pan of lightly salted water to the boil, add the pasta and cook until tender, about 10 minutes, or according to package instructions.

4 Add the sliced sausages to the sauce and cook just until heated through. Drain the pasta, toss it with the sauce and serve.

 Preparation/cooking
10 minutes/18 minutes

Makes 4 portions

Nutritional information
Rich source of beta-carotene, fibre, folate, protein and vitamin B12.

—— Vegetable Lasagne ——

1 tbsp olive oil

1 onion, chopped

2 garlic cloves, crushed

150g (5oz) courgettes, chopped

200g (7oz) aubergines, chopped

150g (5oz) mushrooms, sliced

1 red pepper, chopped

400g (13oz) canned chopped tomatoes

2 tsp mixed dried herbs

1 tbsp tomato purée

90ml (3fl oz) water

salt and pepper, to taste

125g (4oz) broccoli florets

2 x quantities cheese sauce (see page 71)

12 sheets no-precook lasagne

30g (1oz) grated cheese

The whole family will enjoy this vegetarian lasagne. I make it in a fairly deep dish to create plenty of layers.

1 Warm the oil in a frying pan, add the onion and garlic, and sauté for about 1 minute. Add all the vegetables up to and including the red pepper, and sauté, stirring occasionally, for about 5 minutes.

2 Add the chopped tomatoes, mixed herbs, tomato purée and water. Season and then simmer for about 15 minutes. Add the broccoli and cook for 15 minutes, or until all the vegetables are tender. Meanwhile, warm the cheese sauce.

3 To assemble, spoon a third of the vegetables over the base of a 23 x 15 x 7cm (9 x 6 x 3in) ovenproof dish. Cover with 4 overlapping lasagne sheets, then spoon over a third of the cheese sauce. Repeat the layering twice, finishing with a layer of cheese sauce.

4 Sprinkle the grated cheese on top of the final layer of cheese sauce. Transfer to the preheated oven and bake for 40 minutes.

 Preparation/cooking
25 minutes/1 hour
15 minutes

 Oven temperature
180°C/350°F/gas 4

 Makes 8 portions

 Nutritional information
Rich source of beta-carotene, calcium, fibre, protein, B vitamins, incl. B12, and zinc.

 Suitable for freezing

GOLDEN TURKEY FINGERS

250g (8oz) turkey breast fillets

juice of 1 lime or ½ lemon

1 shallot, sliced

plain flour

salt and pepper, to taste

75g (2½oz) dry breadcrumbs

1½ tbsp snipped chives

1 egg, lightly beaten

vegetable oil for shallow frying

1 Cut the turkey into 1cm (½in) strips, removing any skin. Place in a bowl with the lime or lemon juice and shallot. Cover and refrigerate for 30 minutes.

2 Spread some flour on a plate and season with salt and pepper. On another plate, mix together the breadcrumbs and chives. Dip the turkey strips first in the seasoned flour, then in the beaten egg and then in the breadcrumb and chive mixture.

3 Heat the oil in a frying pan, add the turkey strips and sauté until golden and cooked through, about 10 minutes.

 Preparation/cooking
40 minutes/10 minutes

 Makes 4 portions

 Nutritional information
Rich source of folate, protein, B vitamins, incl.B6 and B12, and zinc.

 Suitable for freezing
Uncooked

HEART-SHAPED CHICKEN NUGGETS

375g (12oz) skinless chicken breast fillets, cut into chunks

1 large onion, diced

2 tbsp chopped fresh parsley

1 small apple, peeled and grated

45g (1½oz) fresh white breadcrumbs

1 chicken stock-cube, crumbled

60g (2oz) dry breadcrumbs

60g (2oz) cheese and onion flavour crisps, finely crushed

vegetable oil for frying

The addition of apple gives these nuggets a delicious, moist flavour. If you don't have a heart-shaped cutter, try another shape, but keep to fairly simple lines.

1 Put the first 6 ingredients in a food processor and chop for a few seconds until well combined. Shape the mixture into a flat disc.

2 Use a 6cm (2½in) biscuit cutter to press out heart shapes. Mix together the breadcrumbs and crisps on a plate, and press the pieces into the coating.

3 Heat enough oil for shallow frying in a large frying pan. Add the nuggets and cook for about 6 minutes, turning occasionally, until lightly golden and cooked through.

 Preparation/cooking
25 minutes/6 minutes

 **Makes 8 portions**

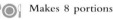 **Nutritional information**
Rich source of protein and B vitamins.

Suitable for freezing

CARAMELISED CHICKEN BREASTS

1 tbsp vegetable oil

1 onion, sliced

1 garlic clove, crushed

salt and pepper, to taste

2 chicken breast fillets

1½ tbsp malt vinegar

1½ tbsp tomato ketchup

1½ tbsp soy sauce

2 tbsp water

1½ tbsp honey

1 Warm the oil in an oven-proof pot, add the onion and garlic, and sauté until soft. Season the chicken, add to the pot and sauté until sealed and golden. Cover, transfer to the preheated oven and cook for 20 minutes, or until tender.

2 Set the chicken aside and place the pot over a high heat. Add the vinegar, bring to the boil and cook for 1 minute, or until reduced by half.

3 Stir in the ketchup, soy sauce and water, and simmer for 2 minutes. Stir in the honey and cook for 2 minutes. Return the chicken to the sauce to heat it through.

 Preparation/cooking
5 minutes/30 minutes

 Oven temperature
180°C/350°F/gas 4

 Makes 4 portions

 Nutritional information
Rich source of folate, protein, B vitamins and zinc.

 Suitable for freezing

TERIYAKI CHICKEN STIR-FRY

300g (10oz) chicken breasts

1½ tbsp vegetable oil

1 small onion, sliced

1 garlic clove, crushed

60g (2oz) baby sweetcorn

60g (2oz) carrots, cut into strips

60g (2oz) cauliflower florets

60g (2oz) courgettes, cut into strips

black pepper, to taste

MARINADE

2 tbsp soy sauce

2 tbsp sake (Japanese rice wine)

½ tsp soft brown sugar

1 tsp sesame oil

1 spring onion, finely chopped

1 Cut the chicken breasts into thin strips. Combine the marinade ingredients in a dish. Add the chicken, and leave to marinate for at least 30 minutes.

2 Heat the vegetable oil in a lidded wok or large frying pan, add the onion and garlic and stir-fry, uncovered, for 2 minutes.

3 Strain the marinade from the chicken and set aside. Add the chicken to the wok and stir-fry until it changes colour. Quarter the baby sweetcorn and add to the wok with the carrots and cauliflower, stir-fry for 3 minutes, then add the courgettes, and continue to stir-fry for 2 minutes.

4 Pour in the marinade. Cover the wok and cook for 2 minutes, or until the vegetables are tender and the chicken is cooked through. Season with a little freshly ground black pepper.

VARIATION

Replace the chicken with 375g (12oz) fillet or rump steak, beaten until tender and cut into strips.

 Preparation/cooking
40 minutes, incl. 30 minutes marinating/ 15 minutes

 Makes 4 portions

 Nutritional information
Rich source of folate, iron, protein, vitamin A, B vitamins, vitamin C and zinc.

— TIP —
For additional flavour, add ¼ teaspoon finely chopped fresh root ginger to the marinade.

CHICKEN CATERPILLAR KEBABS

4 chicken breasts, cubed

425g (14oz) canned lychees

1 red pepper, deseeded and cut into triangles

MARINADE

3 tbsp soy sauce

3 tbsp honey

½ tbsp lemon juice

TO DECORATE

8 spring onion fans (see right)

8 cherry tomatoes or radishes

16 whole cloves

1 Mix together the marinade ingredients in a shallow dish. Add the chicken and leave to marinate for at least 30 minutes. Soak 8 bamboo skewers in water while the chicken marinates.

2 Thread the chicken on to the skewers, putting half a lychee and a red pepper triangle between each piece of chicken. Arrange on a baking tray and transfer to the preheated oven. Cook for about 15 minutes, basting with the marinade and turning them occasionally, until cooked through.

3 To decorate, make a face for each caterpillar using a cherry tomato or radish, studded with clove eyes. Attach it to the tip of the skewer, and thread on a spring onion tail.

 Preparation/cooking
40 minutes, incl. 30 minutes marinating/ 15 minutes

 Oven temperature
180°C/350°F/gas 4

 Makes 8 portions

 Nutritional information
Rich source of beta-carotene, iron, protein, B vitamins, vitamin C and zinc.

— TIP —
To make spring onion fans, cut them into 7cm (3in) lengths. Make 4 slashes at one end. Place in iced water until the ends curl.

ANNABEL'S TASTY MEATBALLS

500g (1lb) lean minced beef

1 onion, finely chopped

1 tbsp chopped fresh parsley

1 chicken stock-cube dissolved in 2 tbsp hot water

1 small apple, peeled and grated

½ tsp Worcestershire sauce

pinch of brown sugar

salt and pepper, to taste

flour for coating

vegetable oil for frying

These meatballs are easy to prepare and delicious (the apple keeps them wonderfully moist). They are good on their own or served with spaghetti and Special Tomato Sauce (see page 122).

1 In a mixing bowl, combine all the ingredients except for the flour and vegetable oil. Use your hands to form the mixture into about 24 walnut-sized balls. Spread the flour on a plate and use to coat the meatballs.

2 Warm the oil in a frying pan, add the meatballs and fry over a high heat for about 3 minutes, until browned on all sides. Lower the heat a little and fry for 12 minutes, or until cooked through.

 Preparation/cooking
10 minutes/15 minutes

 Makes 8 portions

 Nutritional information
Rich source of folate, iron, protein, B vitamins, incl. B12, and zinc.

 Suitable for freezing

HUNGARIAN GOULASH

flour for coating

salt and pepper, to taste

500g (1lb) lean braising steak cut into cubes

2 tbsp vegetable oil

2 onions, peeled and chopped

1 red pepper, deseeded and chopped

250g (8oz) mushrooms, sliced

1 tbsp paprika

400ml (14fl oz) chicken stock (see page 46) or beef stock

3 tbsp tomato purée

1 tbsp tomato ketchup

1 tsp Worcestershire sauce

2 tbsp chopped fresh parsley

6 tbsp sour cream

200g (7oz) pasta noodles, such as tagliateile

For young children, chop the meat and vegetables into small pieces or process in a blender for just a few seconds. Serve with pasta noodles.

1 Spread the flour on a plate, season lightly and use to coat the beef. Warm the vegetable oil in a flameproof casserole dish, add the beef and sauté until browned all over. Remove with a slotted spoon and set aside.

2 Add the onions to the casserole and sauté for 5 minutes. Add the red pepper and sauté for 3–4 minutes, then add the mushrooms and cook for 3 minutes. Sprinkle over the paprika and cook for about 2 minutes.

3 Return the sautéed meat to the dish, pour in the stock and stir in the tomato purée, tomato ketchup, Worcestershire sauce and chopped parsley. Cover, transfer to the preheated oven and cook for about 2 hours. Check that the meat is tender. Season to taste and stir in the sour cream. Set aside and keep warm.

4 Bring a large pan of lightly salted water to the boil, add the noodles and cook until tender, about 8 minutes, or according to package instructions. Drain, arrange a bed of noodles on each plate and top with a serving of goulash.

 Preparation/cooking
15 minutes/2 hours 20 minutes

 Oven temperature
150°C/300°F/gas 2

 Makes 8 portions

 Nutritional information
Rich source of beta-carotene, folate, iron, protein, B vitamins, incl. B12, and zinc.

 Suitable for freezing

STICKY TOFFEE PUDDING

45g (1½oz) butter

140g (4½oz) soft brown sugar

2 eggs

175g (6oz) plain flour, sifted

¼ tsp baking powder

200ml (7fl oz) boiling water

140g (4½oz) stoned dates

¼ tsp bicarbonate of soda

¼ tsp vanilla extract

BUTTERSCOTCH SAUCE

100g (3½oz) soft brown sugar

65g (2¼oz) butter

125ml (4fl oz) double cream

This is one of those classic sticky nursery puddings that never fails to please children and adults alike.

1 Cream together the butter and sugar. Beat the eggs into the mixture, then fold in the flour and baking powder.

2 Pour the boiling water over the dates and add the bicarbonate of soda and vanilla extract. Add this mixture to the batter and blend well.

3 Butter a 28 x 18cm (11 x 7in) ovenproof dish. Pour the batter into the dish and bake in the preheated oven for 40 minutes.

4 To make the sauce, put the brown sugar, butter and cream in a pan and heat gently for about 5 minutes. Remove the pudding from the oven, pour over half the sauce and place under a hot grill until it bubbles Serve the remaining sauce separately.

 Preparation/cooking
10 minutes/40 minutes

 Oven temperature
190°C/375°F/gas 5

 Makes 8 portions

 Nutritional information
Rich source of vitamin B12.

 Suitable for freezing

— TIP —
This can be made in advance, kept in the refrigerator and reheated before serving.

CHOCOLATE ORANGE MINI MUFFINS

125g (4oz) self-raising flour

2 tbsp cocoa powder

125g (4oz) soft margarine

125g (4oz) caster sugar

2 eggs, lightly beaten

grated zest of 1 small orange

60g (2oz) plain chocolate chips

Mini muffins are just the right size for small children. However, if you prefer, you can also bake these in medium muffin trays and they will make about 15 cakes.

1 Sift together the flour and cocoa. Cream the margarine and caster sugar. Add the eggs to the creamed mixture, a little at a time, together with a tablespoon of the flour mixture.

2 Mix in the remaining flour and cocoa until blended. Stir in the orange zest and chocolate chips. Line some muffin trays with paper cases and two-thirds fill each of the cases. Transfer to the preheated oven and cook for 10–12 minutes.

 Preparation/cooking
20 minutes/12 minutes

 Oven temperature
180°C/350°F/gas 4

 Makes 30 mini muffins
or 15 medium muffins

 Nutritional information
Rich source of vitamin B12.

 Suitable for freezing

PIGGY FAIRY CAKE
Use pink-tinted ready-to-roll icing and halved marshmallows to make this animal face, as described below.

HEDGEHOG CAKE
Make a spiky hedgehog with chocolate buttercream icing set with broken flaked chocolate sticks.

CLOWN FACE
Decorate a white-iced cake with yellow grated icing hair, a red icing nose and mouth and black writing icing eyes.

CHARACTER FAIRY CAKES

Decorated fairy cakes are great for parties. Here I describe how to make a piggy face, but you could try clowns, spiky chocolate hedgehogs or ladybirds made with red and black icing. Older children will enjoy helping to decorate these.

125g (4oz) soft margarine

125g (4oz) caster sugar

2 eggs

1 tsp vanilla extract

½ tsp grated lemon zest

125g (4oz) self-raising flour

60g (2oz) raisins or sultanas (optional)

TO DECORATE AS PIGS

pink food colouring

175g (6oz) ready-to-roll white icing, plus icing sugar to dust

3 tbsp apricot jam, sieved and warmed gently

pink marshmallows

coloured writing icing

red liquorice laces

1 Cream together the margarine and sugar until pale and fluffy. Beat in the eggs one at a time then add the vanilla extract and lemon zest.

2 Fold in the flour and raisins, if using, and mix until soft and creamy.

3 Line a bun tray with paper cases and half-fill each case. Transfer to the preheated oven and bake for about 20 minutes. Leave to cool on a wire rack.

4 Knead a little of the pink food colouring into the icing until an even colour tone is achieved. Lightly dust a work surface with icing sugar and roll out the icing until about 2.5mm (⅛in) thick.

5 Use a glass to cut out discs of icing slightly larger than the cakes. Brush the cake tops with a little warmed apricot jam and set the icing on top.

6 Make a pig's snout by attaching a marshmallow, halved across the diameter, to the centre of the cake using jam; draw on nostrils and eyes with writing icing. Add halved marshmallow ears and a short strip of liquorice for the mouth.

 Preparation/cooking
20 minutes/20 minutes plus decorating time

 Oven temperature
180°C/350°F/gas 4

 Makes 15 cakes

 Nutritional information
Rich source of vitamin A and vitamin B12.

 Suitable for freezing
Before decorating

TIP
Ready-to-roll icing can sometimes be bought in a range of colours, but it is easy to tint your own icing by kneading in a few drops of food colouring, as described in step 4.

PARCEL BIRTHDAY CAKE

4 x quantities sponge cake mixture (see Character Fairy Cakes, opposite)

FILLING

250g (8oz) raspberry jam

1 quantity buttercream made with 175g (6oz) soft butter beaten with 375g (12oz) icing sugar, 1 tbsp milk and 1 tsp vanilla extract

TO DECORATE

red, blue, green and yellow food colourings

1.25kg (2½lb) ready-to-roll icing (see left), plus icing sugar to dust

8 tbsp apricot jam, sieved and warmed gently

1 Pour the sponge mixture into a greased and lined 20cm (8in) square tin and a 23 x 12 x 7cm (9 x 5 x 3in) loaf tin. Transfer to the preheated oven and bake the loaf tin for 45 minutes and the square tin for 1 hour. Turn out and leave to cool on a wire rack.

2 Divide the loaf cake into the desired number of blocks to form the small parcels. Slice all the cakes across and sandwich the halves together with a layer each of raspberry jam and buttercream.

3 Choose your colour scheme, then tint the white icing, as described in step 4 of the previous recipe.

4 Brush the top and sides of the cake blocks with apricot jam. Lay the icing over the top, either in a single sheet or in strips for a striped effect. Make icing bows in contrasting colours, sticking them down with jam. Decorate further with icing spots or flowers, or leave plain; or you can even add a few marzipan animals.

 Preparation/cooking
20 minutes/1 hour plus decorating time

 Oven temperature
180°C/350°F/gas 4

 Makes 20 portions

 Nutritional information
Rich source of vitamin A and vitamin B12.

See page 105 for illustration.

SHORTBREAD COOKIES

125g (4oz) butter (cold)

60g (2oz) caster sugar

30g (1oz) ground almonds

pinch of salt

90g (3oz) plain flour, plus flour to dust

60g (2oz) cornflour

glacé icing or icing sugar, to decorate (optional)

1 Beat together the butter and sugar until fluffy. Add the remaining ingredients and beat until the mixture sticks together and begins to form a ball.

2 Dust a pastry board with flour, turn out the mixture, and knead gently for 1–2 minutes to form a smooth dough. Roll the dough out until 5mm (¼in) thick. Cut into shapes using biscuit cutters.

3 Using a palette knife, transfer the shapes to a greased baking sheet. Bake in the preheated oven for 15 minutes, or until lightly golden. Leave to cool on the tray, then lift off. Ice or decorate, as desired.

 Preparation/cooking
15 minutes/15 minutes

 Oven temperature
180°C/350°F/gas 4

 Makes 12–15 cookies

 Nutritional information
Rich source of vitamin A.

 Suitable for freezing

See page 121 for further illustration.

3-5
Years

ONCE YOUR CHILD BEGINS TO INTERACT
MORE WITH HER PEERS, PERHAPS WHEN SHE
STARTS NURSERY OR SCHOOL, YOU MAY FIND YOU
NO LONGER HAVE COMPLETE CONTROL OVER
WHAT SHE EATS. HOWEVER, IF YOU CONTINUE TO
ENCOURAGE HER TO EAT A VARIED DIET AT
HOME AND KEEP INTRODUCING NEW AND
EXCITING RECIPES, YOU WILL HAVE A
HAPPY, HEALTHY EATER.

A menu planner for each age-group begins on page 132

The Pre-school Child

THE GREATEST CHANGE in your child's life at this stage of development will probably be starting nursery school, and at this point, eating has to fit into more of a routine. Nursery-age children will need a good breakfast to keep them alert until lunchtime. Packed lunches may soon become an essential part of your child's diet too, and they will need to be nutritious and sustaining. This is an exciting age: your child will be learning new skills, and it is the perfect time to consolidate good eating habits, encourage diversity and involve children in cooking.

A healthy and varied diet

Between the ages of 3 and 5 your child's manual dexterity should greatly improve and she should be able to master all the basic eating skills. She should also have her first full set of teeth. Around this age many children will start noticing commercials that push unhealthy foods. This is a good time to explain the basic principles of nutrition to your child.

If parents proffer fresh fruit and vegetables in a defensive or apologetic way, children will begin to reject them. So if you can make these fresh foods seem to be the appealing, tasty foods they really are, then your child will not equate "healthy" with "nasty". Vitamin pills are no substitute for fresh fruit and vegetables in your child's diet.

AVOIDING PROBLEMS

Children are great mimics and will be affected by adult attitudes to eating. If parents do not eat healthily themselves, or refuse to try new dishes, children are likely to copy their conservative eating habits. If a member of the family is slimming, don't discuss it in front of the children. You need to avoid creating eating anxieties.

The good breakfast guide

Nutritionists generally agree that an adequate breakfast is necessary for proper physical and mental functioning. Many children have their last meal around 5 p.m. and may not eat until 7 a.m. the next day. They will have fasted for

14 hours and their brain will need a kick start to prepare for the demands of the day ahead. A wholegrain cereal is best, such as wheat biscuits (see page 12). Alternatively, offer wholemeal toast with an egg or cheese.

FRUIT & JUICE

Offer a variety of fresh and dried fruits, and add them to milkshakes and cereals. Try serving fruit in new ways: put half a kiwi in an egg cup so your child can scoop out the flesh with a teaspoon.

PORRIDGE
WITH JAM

BOILED EGG
AND TOAST

CEREAL
WITH MILK

MUESLI, FRUIT
AND YOGURT

ORANGE
JUICE

Outside the home

Some time after her third birthday, if not well before, your child may be looked after by a childminder or a nursery school. If lunch is provided, check that it is well-balanced and nutritious. Where a picnic lunch is required, try to make it interesting and healthy. Young children like miniature portions, so individual cheeses, tiny boxes of raisins or mini muffins are useful additions.

PICNIC FOOD
Portions should be easy to eat and not too messy.

A chicken drumstick is ideal for lunch

PACKING PORTABLE FOODS

Warm conditions encourage the growth of bacteria so it's essential to keep picnic lunches cool, especially if you have included cooked meats. An insulated box with an ice pack would be ideal, or a small carton of frozen juice can be packed with sandwiches to keep them cool. By the time your child is ready to eat lunch, the juice should have defrosted.

BRIEFING CARERS

If you find that your child is always over-hungry when she comes out of pre-school, ask a teacher or carer to monitor what she eats and report back to you. Children are usually quite hungry after a pre-school day and it can be a good time to encourage them to snack healthily. You can bring a nutritious snack, such as a banana or a cheese and tomato sandwich when you collect your child, and you will usually find that she will eat it eagerly. If you have a policy of no sweets or chocolates between meals, then let carers and relatives know so that you can be consistent with your rules. You might suggest other treats, such as exotic fruits or homemade biscuits.

It may not be a good idea to ban sweets altogether, because there is a danger of making them into an even more desirable "forbidden fruit". It is probably easier to limit sweets to certain times, such as after meals and at weekends.

FAST FOOD

Children are eating more "fast food" than ever before. Many of these foods are high in calories, salt or sugar but low in nutrients. To encourage young fast food addicts to eat a nutritious diet, make healthy versions of their fast food favourites, such as Mini Pizzas (see page 91), Crunchy Chicken Fingers (see page 96), Oven-baked Chips (see page 125), and Ice Lollipops (see page 99).

REMEMBER

◆ ENSURE THAT YOUR CHILD eats a substantial breakfast, particularly on weekdays if she will be at nursery or pre-school. If she is a very slow eater and you are short of time, give her a sandwich or healthy muffin to eat on the way.

◆ ENSURE THAT FOOD in your child's picnic lunch is kept cool and well-wrapped so that it stays free from bacteria.

◆ WHEN SETTING UP a healthy eating plan, enlist the help of visitors, grandparents and other carers. If everyone is aware of your food policies, your child will be treated consistently.

International Tastes

TRY TO INTRODUCE EXCITING FLAVOURS and new dishes periodically so that your child's tastes and horizons are continually broadened and enriched. Many children are eager to experience new foods at this age, and there are wonderful dishes from all around the world that make easy family meals. It may even give you the opportunity to talk with your child about different countries and their cultures.

An all-in-one vibrant rice dish

SLEEPING CANNELLONI
Introduce this Italian classic with a few decorative touches that will add instant child appeal. The stuffed cannelloni tubes have the usual "blanket" of cheese sauce but little mushroom faces and black olive boots carry the theme to a humorous point. (See page 122 for recipe.)

Use freshly grated cheese to make the hair and decorate with pepper bows

A band of tomato sauce makes a quick turned down "sheet"

VEGETABLE SAMOSAS
These crispy Indian-style parcels hide a filling of mildly spiced chopped vegetables. They are good as a hot or cold snack. (See page 124 for recipe.)

Crunchy corn taco shells are an excellent store cupboard stand-by

BEEF TACOS

Crispy corn tacos stuffed with minced beef or chicken strips, beans and salad are popular with children. The filling in these tacos has a hint of chilli and coriander to give it a little kick. (See page 129 for recipe.)

An irresistible combination of ingredients that is fun to eat

PAELLA

Give supper a Spanish flavour with this festive one-pot meal of chicken, sausages, prawns and vibrant yellow rice. (See page 126 for recipe.)

Crisp filo pastry

SINGAPORE NOODLES

Curly Chinese noodles, chicken and prawns stir-fried with soy sauce, sake and sesame oil combine to create a fast supper dish that is bursting with flavours. (See page 128 for recipe.)

SLEEPING CANNELLONI

250g (8oz) frozen leaf spinach

30g (1oz) butter

1 onion, finely chopped

1 small garlic clove, crushed

125g (4oz) mushrooms, sliced

1 tbsp flour

90ml (3fl oz) milk

2 tbsp thick single cream

salt and pepper, to taste

8 no-precook cannelloni tubes

CHEESE SAUCE

30g (1oz) butter

30g (1oz) flour

450ml (¾ pint) milk

60g (2oz) each grated Gruyère and Cheddar cheese

½ tsp mustard powder

salt and pepper, to taste

TO DECORATE

ready-made tomato sauce (e.g. passata), 8 sautéed button mushrooms, handful of grated Cheddar, 8 black olives, tiny green pepper bows and squares and red pepper strips

1 Place the spinach in a pan without water, cover, set over a low heat and cook gently for 5 minutes, or according to package instructions. Squeeze out any excess water.

2 Warm the butter in a pan, add the onion and garlic and sauté until softened. Add the mushrooms and cook for 5 minutes. Stir in the flour and cook for 1 minute. Add the cooked spinach, stir in the milk and cook for 2 minutes. Remove the pan from the heat, stir in the cream and season to taste.

3 Lightly grease a 25 x 20cm (10 x 8in) ovenproof dish. Use a teaspoon to push the stuffing into the cannelloni tubes then arrange them in the dish in a single layer.

4 To make the sauce, melt the butter in a pan over a low heat, add the flour and stir to make a paste. Cook gently for 2 minutes, then whisk in the milk and cook, stirring, until thickened. Remove from the heat, stir in the cheeses until melted, add the mustard powder and season to taste.

5 Pour the sauce over the cannelloni, transfer to the preheated oven and bake for 30 minutes.

6 To decorate, use the tomato sauce to make a turned-down sheet and arrange the olives as feet. Make slits in the mushrooms, push in green pepper eyes and red pepper mouths, and use the grated cheese as hair, adding the green pepper bows.

 Preparation/cooking
35 minutes/45 minutes

 Oven temperature
180°C/350°F/gas 4

 Makes 8 portions

 Nutritional information
Rich source of beta-carotene, calcium, folate, iron, protein, B vitamins, incl. B12, and zinc.

 Suitable for freezing
Undecorated

See page 120 for main illustration.

SPECIAL TOMATO SAUCE

1 tsp olive oil

1 garlic clove, chopped

400g (13oz) canned tomatoes

2 tbsp red pesto

¼ tsp mild chilli powder

1 tsp balsamic vinegar

1 tsp caster sugar

salt and pepper, to taste

1 tbsp shredded fresh basil

2 tbsp freshly grated Parmesan

This full-flavoured tomato sauce is wonderfully versatile: try it as a base for pizza topping, or add a few mini meatballs or a small can of tuna to make a simple pasta sauce.

1 Heat the oil in a frying pan over a low heat, add the garlic and sauté for 30 seconds. Stir in the tomatoes and break them up with a spoon. Add the remaining ingredients except the basil and Parmesan. Season then simmer gently for 10 minutes.

2 Stir in the basil and Parmesan, and cook just until the cheese has melted.

 Preparation/cooking
5 minutes/12 minutes

 Makes 4 portions

 Nutritional information
Rich source of beta-carotene, calcium, protein and B vitamins.

 Suitable for freezing

PASTA TWISTS WITH COURGETTES

1 tbsp olive oil

1 small onion, sliced

1 garlic clove, chopped

125g (4oz) courgettes, sliced

100g (3½oz) mushrooms, sliced

300ml (½ pint) passata

½ tsp balsamic vinegar

½ tsp sugar

salt and pepper, to taste

200g (7oz) pasta twists (fusilli)

30g (1oz) freshly grated
Parmesan

Another quick recipe that will encourage children to enjoy eating vegetables. Vary the vegetables according to seasonal availability.

1 Heat the oil in a pan, add the onion, garlic, courgettes and mushrooms, and cook for 7–8 minutes. Stir in the passata, vinegar and sugar, and season to taste. Simmer, covered, for 15 minutes.

2 Meanwhile, bring a pan of lightly salted water to the boil and cook the pasta until tender, about 10 minutes, or according to package instructions.

3 Remove the sauce from the heat, stir in the Parmesan then toss with the drained pasta.

 Preparation/cooking
10 minutes/25 minutes

 Makes 4 portions

 Nutritional information
Rich source of calcium,
fibre and protein.

✳ **Suitable for freezing**

ITALIAN RISOTTO WITH MUSHROOMS & PEAS

2 tbsp vegetable oil

1 onion, chopped

1 garlic clove, crushed

60g (2oz) red pepper,
deseeded and chopped

100g (3½oz) button
mushrooms, sliced

200g (7oz) risotto rice
(arborio, carnaroli or vialone)

900ml (1½ pints) hot
vegetable stock or chicken
stock (see page 46)

100g (3½oz) frozen peas

30g (1oz) freshly grated
Parmesan

knob of butter

salt and pepper, to taste

To make a good risotto, you need a heavy-based pan that will allow even, slow cooking: a large, fairly deep frying pan is ideal.

1 Heat the oil in a pan over a medium-low heat. Add the onion and garlic and cook for 1 minute. Add the pepper and mushrooms and cook for 5 minutes.

2 Add the rice and cook, stirring continuously, for 1 minute, until all the grains are well coated with oil. Pour in a ladleful of hot stock and simmer, stirring constantly, until absorbed.

3 Continue to add small quantities of hot stock, waiting for each ladleful to be absorbed before adding more. Stir frequently to prevent sticking.

4 When all the stock has been added and the rice is almost cooked, about 20–25 minutes, stir in the peas and cook for 3–4 minutes. Stir in the Parmesan and butter, season to taste, and serve.

VARIATION

Omit the peas and add 125g (4oz) cooked, finely sliced ham just before adding the Parmesan.

 Preparation/cooking
10 minutes/40 minutes

 Makes 4 portions

Nutritional information
Rich source of beta-carotene,
calcium, folate and protein.

— TIP —
If you want to prepare the risotto in advance, only add half the stock and remove from the heat. Add the remaining stock gradually and continue to cook just before you want to serve the risotto.

MILDLY SPICED VEGETABLE SAMOSAS

½ tbsp vegetable oil

½ onion, very finely chopped

½ garlic clove, crushed

¼ tsp each curry powder,
ground ginger and
ground cumin

75g (2½oz) button
mushrooms, finely chopped

90g (3oz) cauliflower, cut
into very small florets

1 carrot, very finely chopped

2 tsp caster sugar

3 tsp natural yogurt

salt and pepper, to taste

1 packet filo pastry sheets

60g (2oz) butter, melted

1 Heat the oil in a frying pan, add the onion and garlic and sauté for 2–3 minutes. Stir in the spices and sauté for 1 minute. Add the vegetables and cook for 5 minutes, stirring occasionally. Stir in the sugar and yogurt. Season and cook for 3–4 minutes.

2 Lay the filo pastry out flat and cover with a damp tea towel. Place one sheet of pastry on the work surface and brush with melted butter. Fold the pastry in half lengthways and brush again with butter.

3 Place a tablespoon of filling on one end of the strip, leaving a 2.5cm (1in) wide border around it. Fold over the corner to make a triangle, then keep folding the parcel over on itself, along the length of the pastry. Seal the flap left at the end with melted butter. Repeat with the remaining pastry and filling.

4 Place the samosas on a lightly greased baking sheet and brush with more butter. Bake in the preheated oven for 20–25 minutes, or until crisp.

 Preparation/cooking
35 minutes/35 minutes

 Oven temperature
180°C/350°F/gas 4

 Makes 8 portions

 Nutritional information
Rich source of beta-carotene.

 Suitable for freezing
Uncooked

— TIP —
When handling filo pastry, keep the piece you are not working with covered with a damp tea towel to prevent it from drying out and becoming brittle and difficult to work with.

MINI BEAN & VEGGIE ENCHILADAS

1 tbsp vegetable oil

½ onion, chopped

1 small garlic clove, crushed

¼ red chilli, finely chopped (optional)

200g (7oz) canned red kidney beans or refried beans

125g (4oz) cooked sweetcorn

200g (7oz) canned chopped tomatoes, drained

salt and pepper, to taste

1 tbsp chopped fresh parsley

4 mini flour tortillas

45g (1½oz) grated Cheddar cheese

Small flour tortillas (soft Mexican flatbreads) can be bought and filled with a variety of ingredients. Kidney beans are a good protein source.

1 Heat the oil in a frying pan, add the onion, garlic and chilli if using, and cook gently for 3 minutes.

2 Roughly chop the kidney beans. Add the beans to the frying pan with the sweetcorn and chopped tomatoes. Season to taste and cook over a medium heat for 5 minutes. Sprinkle with parsley.

3 Divide the filling among the tortillas, roll them up and top with cheese. Heat through in a microwave for 1–2 minutes, or in a conventional oven for 6 minutes, then grill until golden and bubbly.

VARIATION

Replace the beans with 2 chicken breasts, cut into strips, seasoned and fried. Replace the sweetcorn and tomatoes with half a small red pepper, chopped and sautéed. Heat the enchiladas through then dress with a spoonful each of salsa and sour cream.

 Preparation/cooking 10 minutes/15 minutes

 Oven temperature microwave on high or conventional oven at 180°C/350°F/gas 4

 Makes 4 portions

 Nutritional information Rich source of beta-carotene, calcium, fibre, folate, iron, protein, vitamin C and zinc.

FISH & OVEN-BAKED CHIPS

350g (11½oz) small–medium potatoes, scrubbed

3½ tbsp olive oil

freshly ground sea salt and pepper, to taste

flour, to coat

250g (8oz) plaice or cod fillets, cut into chunks

1 lightly beaten egg

1 x 30g (1oz) bag ready-salted crisps, crushed

If you are making these for a special children's tea, why not serve them in a cone made from a rolled-up comic?

1 Halve the potatoes lengthways then cut each piece into 4 sticks. Pour 1½ tablespoons of oil into a roasting tin and place in the preheated oven for 2–3 minutes.

2 Transfer the potatoes to the roasting tin. Toss in the oil until well coated and sprinkle with sea salt. Return to the oven and bake for 30 minutes, or until crisp on the outside but tender.

3 Meanwhile, season the flour and use to coat the fish pieces, then dip them in egg, and roll in the crisps. Heat the remaining oil in a frying pan, add the fish and cook thoroughly. Serve with the chips.

 Preparation/cooking 5 minutes/35 minutes

 Oven temperature 200°C/400°F/gas 6

 Makes 4 portions

 Nutritional information Rich source of folate, protein, vitamin B12 and vitamin E.

TIP
The fish can be fried in advance and then reheated in the oven. It can also be baked on a greased baking tray for 10–12 minutes.

STICKY BAR-B-Q DRUMSTICKS

4 large chicken drumsticks, scored with a knife (remove the skin first if preferred)

MARINADE

½ tbsp vegetable oil

1 small onion, chopped

75g (2½oz) dark muscovado sugar

juice of ½ lemon

½ tbsp Worcestershire sauce

4 tbsp tomato ketchup

1 tbsp white wine vinegar

Barbecued drumsticks are excellent eaten hot off the grill or cold in lunch boxes. Wrap the drumstick ends in foil so that they can be eaten with the fingers.

1 To make the marinade, heat the oil in a frying pan, add the onion and sauté until soft. Stir in the sugar and cook gently for 1–2 minutes. Add the remaining ingredients and simmer for 5 minutes.

2 Pour the mixture into a glass or ceramic bowl, add the drumsticks, and marinate for at least 30 minutes and up to 12 hours.

3 Transfer the drumsticks to a baking dish, baste well and place under a preheated grill. Cook for 20 minutes, turning halfway through and basting with the barbecue sauce. Check they are cooked through, wrap the ends in foil, and serve hot or cold.

 Preparation/cooking
45 minutes, incl.
30 minutes marinating/
20 minutes

 Makes 4 portions

 Nutritional information
Rich source of protein and B vitamins.

❄ **Suitable for freezing**

PAELLA

1 tbsp sunflower oil

1 onion, chopped

2 boneless chicken breasts, cut into chunks

1 red pepper, deseeded and chopped

300g (10oz) long-grain rice

1 tsp turmeric

1 tsp mild chilli powder

2 celery sticks, chopped

1 litre (1¾ pints) chicken stock (see page 46)

1 bay leaf

100g (3½oz) frozen peas

2 pork sausages, grilled

100g (3½oz) small cooked peeled prawns

salt and pepper, to taste

This is a great all-in-one dish that's easy to cook and full of flavour. The turmeric gives the rice a rich yellow tint.

1 Heat the oil in a deep, heavy-based frying pan, add the onion and sauté for 1 minute. Add the chicken and sauté until sealed on all sides.

2 Add the red pepper and cook, stirring, for 1 minute. Stir in the rice, turmeric, chilli powder and celery, and sauté for 1 minute, stirring the mixture constantly.

3 Pour in the stock, add the bay leaf, stir well, then leave to simmer for 15–20 minutes, uncovered, until all the liquid is absorbed.

4 Add the peas to the pan and cook for 2–3 minutes. Slice the sausages on the diagonal and then add to the rice with the prawns and seasoning. Allow to heat through, remove the bay leaf, and serve.

 Preparation/cooking
10 minutes/25 minutes

 Makes 8 portions

 Nutritional information
Rich source of beta-carotene, folate, protein, vitamin E and zinc.

 Suitable for freezing

See page 120 for illustration.

CHICKEN SATAY

2 chicken breasts, cut into chunks

MARINADE

2 tbsp yellow bean sauce

2 tbsp soy sauce

2 tbsp peanut butter

1 tbsp rice wine vinegar

2 tbsp honey

Thread vegetable chunks, perhaps pieces of onion or pepper, onto the skewers, if liked.

1 Mix all the marinade ingredients with the chicken in a glass or ceramic bowl. Leave to marinate for at least 30 minutes. Soak 4 bamboo skewers in water while the chicken marinates.

2 Thread the chicken on to the skewers and cook under a preheated grill for 8–10 minutes until cooked through, turning and basting occasionally with the marinade.

 Preparation/cooking
35 minutes, incl.
30 minutes marinating/
10 minutes

 Makes 4 portions

 Nutritional information
Rich source of iron, protein, B vitamins and zinc.

—— NOTE ——
Remove the skewers before serving to young children.

EGG-FRIED RICE WITH CHICKEN & PRAWNS

175g (6oz) basmati rice, rinsed in cold water then drained

4 tbsp vegetable oil

1 small onion, finely chopped

60g (2oz) red pepper, deseeded and finely chopped

salt and pepper, to taste

1 beaten egg

60g (2oz) frozen peas

60g (2oz) frozen sweetcorn

1 large spring onion, sliced

1 chicken breast, cut into thin strips

125g (4oz) cooked prawns (optional)

1 tbsp light soy sauce

Egg-fried rice with vegetables and chicken is an appealing, simple meal. Your child may be keen to practise eating with chopsticks; it will be slow going at first so provide a fork as well.

1 Bring a pan of lightly salted water to the boil, add the rice and cook until tender, about 10 minutes.

2 Heat half the oil in a large frying pan or wok, add the onion and sauté for 2 minutes. Add the red pepper and cook for 7–8 minutes. Season the beaten egg with a little pepper, pour it into the pan, tipping the pan to spread it evenly, and cook until set. Remove from the heat and break the egg up into small pieces with a wooden spatula.

3 Return the pan to the heat, add the peas and sweetcorn and cook until tender. Remove the egg/vegetable mixture from the pan, and set aside. Add the remaining oil and sauté the spring onion for 1 minute. Add the shredded chicken and sauté for 3–4 minutes, or until cooked, then season.

4 Add the cooked rice and prawns, if using, and toss the rice over a high heat for 2 minutes. Return the egg/vegetable mixture to the pan, add the soy sauce and toss together until heated through.

 Preparation/cooking
10 minutes/30 minutes

 Makes 4 portions

 Nutritional information
Rich source of beta-carotene, folate, protein, vitamin B12, vitamin C and zinc.

 Suitable for freezing

Your child can begin to learn about different cultures and their traditions, but it may be a while before he masters the art of using chopsticks

Singapore Noodles

150g (5oz) chicken breast

2½ tbsp vegetable oil

1 beaten egg

1 garlic clove, chopped

¼ tsp finely chopped red chilli (optional)

75g (2½oz) baby sweetcorn

75g (2½oz) each carrots and courgettes, cut into thin strips

75g (2½oz) beansprouts

¼ tsp mild curry powder

4 tbsp strong chicken stock

90g (3oz) small peeled prawns

3 spring onions, thinly sliced

150g (5oz) Chinese noodles

MARINADE

1 tbsp each soy sauce and sake

½ tsp sugar

1 tsp cornflour

These noodles can be made spicier with added chilli and curry powder. If preferred, replace the prawns with pork or more chicken. For extra flavour, fry the beaten egg in ½ tablespoon of sesame oil.

1 Mix together the marinade ingredients in a bowl, cut the chicken into thin strips, add to the bowl and marinate for at least 30 minutes.

2 Heat ½ tablespoon of oil in a frying pan, add the egg and fry to make a thin omelette. Remove from the pan and cut into ribbons. Heat a tablespoon of oil in the pan or a wok and sauté the garlic and chilli, if using, for 30 seconds. Drain the chicken, add to the pan and cook for 3–4 minutes, then set aside.

3 Heat the remaining oil in the wok. Add the baby sweetcorn and carrots and stir-fry for 2 minutes. Add the courgettes and beansprouts and cook for 2 minutes. Stir the curry powder into the stock and add to the wok. Return the chicken to the pan with the prawns, spring onions and egg, and fry for 2 minutes.

4 Cook the noodles in a pan of boiling water for 3 minutes, or according to package instructions. Drain, mix with the stir-fry and heat through.

 Preparation/cooking
45 minutes, incl. 30 minutes marinating/20 minutes

 Makes 4 portions

 Nutritional information
Rich source of beta-carotene, fibre, folate, iron, protein, B vitamins, incl. B12, vitamin C and zinc.

See page 121 for main illustration.

Beef Stir-fry with Oyster Sauce

375g (12oz) lean beef frying steak, cut into strips

1 tbsp corn oil

1 small onion, sliced

1 tbsp sesame oil

1 garlic clove, crushed

1 carrot, cut into strips or stars

125g (4oz) broccoli florets

125g (4oz) baby sweetcorn

125g (4oz) mangetout

1 red pepper, cut into strips

MARINADE

1 tbsp each sake and oyster sauce

2 tbsp soy sauce

1 tsp light brown sugar

This quick Oriental dish uses oyster sauce, but there are other good, ready-made stir-fry sauces available – check they are additive-free.

1 Combine the marinade ingredients in a bowl. Add the beef strips and marinate for 30 minutes. Remove the beef and set aside, reserving the marinade.

2 Meanwhile, heat the corn oil in a wok or frying pan. Add half the onion and stir-fry until softened. Add the beef and stir-fry until cooked, then remove and set aside.

3 Heat the sesame oil in the wok and stir-fry the remaining onion and the garlic for 2–3 minutes. Add the carrot, broccoli and sweetcorn, and stir-fry for 3–4 minutes. Add the mangetout and red pepper, then stir-fry for a further 3–4 minutes.

4 Return the beef strips to the pan, pour in the marinade and stir-fry for 2–3 minutes more.

 Preparation/cooking
45 minutes, incl. 30 minutes marinating/25 minutes

 Makes 4 portions

 Nutritional information
Rich source of beta-carotene, fibre, folate, iron, protein, B vitamins, incl. B12, vitamin C and zinc.

 Suitable for freezing

Beef Teriyaki Skewers

3 tbsp soy sauce

4 tbsp mirin (sweet rice wine)

1 tsp sesame oil

1 garlic clove, crushed

2.5cm (1in) piece
fresh root ginger, grated

300g (10oz) fillet steak, cubed

1 tsp cornflour

1 Combine all the ingredients except the cornflour in a bowl and marinate for at least 1 hour. Soak 4 bamboo skewers in water while the steak marinates.

2 Thread the beef on to the skewers, reserving the marinade. Transfer the skewers to the grill or barbecue and cook for 4–5 minutes on each side.

3 Meanwhile, mix the cornflour to a paste with 1 tablespoon of the marinade then pour into a pan with the remaining marinade. Heat for 2 minutes, or until thickened. Serve as a dipping sauce.

 Preparation/cooking
1 hour 5 minutes, incl.
1 hour marinating/
10 minutes

 Makes 4 portions

 Nutritional information
Rich source of iron,
protein, B vitamins, incl.
B12, and zinc.

Beef Tacos

125g (4oz) lean minced beef

½ small onion, finely diced

½ each red and green
pepper, cored, deseeded
and finely diced

100g (3½oz) canned red
kidney beans

1 tomato, skinned, deseeded
and diced

½ tbsp mild chilli sauce

½ tbsp chopped fresh coriander

salt and pepper, to taste

4 taco shells

4 lettuce leaves

1 Heat a dry frying pan for 1 minute. Add the minced beef and stir-fry for about 5 minutes, or until cooked through. Add the onion and cook for 2 minutes. Add the red and green peppers, and sauté for a further 2 minutes. Stir in the beans, tomato, chilli sauce and half the coriander. Cook gently for 3–4 minutes. Season to taste.

2 Meanwhile, warm the tacos in the preheated oven for 2–3 minutes, or in a microwave on full power for 1 minute. Remove from the oven, line with the lettuce, spoon in the beef mixture and garnish with the remaining coriander.

 Preparation/cooking
10 minutes/15 minutes

 Oven temperature
180°C/350°F/gas 4

 Makes 4 portions

 Nutritional information
Rich source of beta-carotene,
fibre, folate, iron, protein,
vitamin B12, vitamin C
and zinc.

COUNTRY APPLE CAKE

A crumbly-textured dark apple cake that is perfect for tea.

375g (12oz) self-raising flour

2 tsp mixed spice

175g (6oz) butter

300g (10oz) cooking apples, peeled, cored and chopped

250g (8oz) sultanas

150ml (¼ pint) milk

175g (6oz) light muscovado sugar

1 egg, lightly beaten

2 tbsp honey

½ tbsp granulated sugar

1 Sift the flour and mixed spice into a bowl and rub in the butter using your fingertips.

2 Combine the apples, sultanas, milk and muscovado sugar, and stir into the flour mixture. Stir in the beaten egg.

3 Line a 20cm (8in) round cake tin. Spoon the mixture into the tin. Bake in the preheated oven for 1 hour. Remove, leave in the tin for 10 minutes, then transfer to a wire rack to cool.

4 Melt the honey in a small pan and use to brush the top of the cake, then sprinkle with the granulated sugar. Store in an airtight container.

Preparation/cooking
25 minutes/1 hour

Oven temperature
170°C/325°F/gas 3

Makes 8 portions

Nutritional information
Rich source of calcium, fibre, iron, vitamin A and vitamin B12.

Suitable for freezing

CHOCOLATE CHIP & ORANGE CUT-OUT COOKIES

Children love interestingly shaped biscuits and will enjoy helping you cut out these biscuits. The subtle orange flavour combines well with the chocolate chips to make these very "moreish".

175g (6oz) butter (at room temperature)

75g (2½oz) icing sugar, sieved

225g (7½oz) self-raising flour, sieved

½ tsp salt

½ tsp grated orange zest

60g (2oz) plain chocolate chips

1 Put all the ingredients except the chocolate chips in a food processor and mix until blended together (alternatively, beat together by hand).

2 Mix in the chocolate chips by hand. Knead the dough until pliable, form into a ball, wrap in clingfilm and set aside in the fridge for about 1 hour.

3 Roll out the dough to a thickness of ½cm (¼in) and cut into shapes using a variety of cookie cutters. Arrange on a lightly greased baking tray (or one sprayed with non-stick cooking spray) and bake in the preheated oven for about 10 minutes.

Preparation/cooking
1 hour 15 minutes, incl. 1 hour chilling/ 10 minutes

Oven temperature
180°C/350°F/gas 4

Makes 25–30 cookies

Nutritional information
Rich source of vitamin A.

Suitable for freezing

— CHOCOLATE PROFITEROLES & CHOUX PASTRY MICE

CHOUX PASTRY

90g (3oz) lightly salted butter, cut into small pieces

200ml (7fl oz) water

90g (3oz) plain flour

3 eggs, lightly beaten

CREAM FILLING

600ml (1 pint) double cream

2 tbsp icing sugar

CHOCOLATE ICING

175g (6oz) high-quality plain chocolate, broken into small pieces

90g (3oz) unsalted butter, cut into small pieces

TO DECORATE AS MICE (OPTIONAL)

flaked almonds

chocolate chips

glacé cherries

red liquorice laces

1 To make the pastry, put the butter and water in a saucepan and slowly bring to the boil. Remove from the heat and sift in the flour, then stir to combine. Beat the mixture vigorously with a wooden spoon until it comes away from the sides of the saucepan then allow to cool a little.

2 Add the eggs, a little at a time, until the mixture is soft and smooth and has a dropping consistency (you may not need to add all the egg).

3 Fit a size 8 plain round nozzle into a piping bag and pipe small round mounds of the mixture on to a greased baking sheet. Bake in the preheated oven for 20–25 minutes. Remove and leave to cool.

4 Whisk the double cream with the icing sugar until thick and fluffy. Cut a slit in the profiteroles and fill with the sweetened cream.

5 Melt the chocolate in a heatproof bowl set over a saucepan of simmering water, or in a microwave on full power for 1 minute. Stir in the butter, allow to melt and combine to make a smooth mixture. Leave to cool slightly.

6 Spread a little of the chocolate mixture over the top of each profiterole with a palette knife. If liked, the profiteroles can be decorated to look like mice: add a pair of flaked almond ears, a chocolate chip nose, glacé cherry eyes and a red liquorice tail.

 Preparation/cooking
10 minutes/35 minutes plus decoration

 Oven temperature
200°C/400°F/gas 6

 Makes 20 profiteroles

 Nutritional information
Rich source of vitamin A.

 Suitable for freezing
Undecorated

TIP
The pastry will expand during cooking, so do not make the pastry for the profiterole mice longer than 1½ inches.

— CHEWY APRICOT & CHOCOLATE CEREAL BARS —

150g (5oz) rolled oats

50g (1½oz) puffed rice (rice crispies)

100g (3½oz) dried apricots, chopped

60g (2oz) pecan nuts, chopped (optional)

100g (3½oz) unsalted butter

125g (4oz) golden syrup

85g (2½oz) white (or plain) chocolate, broken into pieces

These are great for special treats and are popular with adults and children. They are fun for children to make themselves as they require no oven cooking.

1 Combine the oats, puffed rice, chopped apricots and nuts (if using) in a mixing bowl.

2 Put the butter and golden syrup in a small saucepan and heat gently. Add the chocolate and stir until melted. Stir the mixture into the dry ingredients until they are well coated.

3 Press the mixture into a shallow 28 x 18cm (11 x 7in) lined tin using a potato masher to level the surface. Store in the fridge to set. Cut into bars and keep these in the fridge.

 Preparation
15 minutes plus refrigeration time

 Makes 10 portions

 Nutritional information
Rich source of fibre, folate, iron, vitamin A and vitamin B12.

TIP
A handy tip for measuring the amount of syrup needed is first to weigh the whole tin and then spoon out as much syrup as necessary to decrease the weight shown by 150g (5oz).

MENUS: 4–6 months

START WITH ONE MEAL of solids a day, building up to three
solid meals a day by week five or six, when a third solid meal
should be introduced at tea or supper time. It can be a good
idea to offer half the usual milk feed before the solids, then
finish the meal with milk (see page 24). Some babies may need
an extra milk feed or a little cooled boiled water during the day.

WEEKS 1&2	EARLY A.M.	BREAKFAST	LUNCH	MID P.M.	BEDTIME
DAY 1	MILK	MILK	MILK FIRST FRUIT PURÉE (APPLE) *see page 29*	MILK	MILK
DAY 2	MILK	MILK	MILK FIRST VEG PURÉE (CARROT) *see page 28*	MILK	MILK
DAY 3	MILK	MILK	MILK FRUITY BABY RICE (PEAR) *see page 29*	MILK	MILK
DAY 4	MILK	MILK	MILK FIRST VEG PURÉE (POTATO) *see page 28*	MILK	MILK
DAY 5	MILK	MILK	MILK FIRST FRUIT PURÉE (APPLE) *see page 29*	MILK	MILK
DAY 6	MILK	MILK	MILK SWEET POTATO PURÉE *see page 30*	MILK	MILK
DAY 7	MILK	MILK	MILK MASHED BANANA *see page 29*	MILK	MILK

WEEKS 3&4	EARLY A.M.	BREAKFAST	LUNCH	MID P.M.	BEDTIME
DAY 1	MILK	MILK FRUITY BABY RICE (PEAR) *see page 29*	MILK FIRST VEG PURÉE (CARROT) *see page 28*	MILK	MILK
DAY 2	MILK	MILK FIRST FRUIT PURÉE (APPLE) *see page 29*	MILK FIRST VEG PURÉE (POTATO) *see page 28*	MILK	MILK
DAY 3	MILK	MILK DRIED APRICOT & BABY RICE *see page 31*	MILK FIRST VEG PURÉE (SWEDE) *see page 28*	MILK	MILK
DAY 4	MILK	MILK MASHED BANANA *see page 29*	MILK FIRST VEG PURÉE (PARSNIP) *see page 28*	MILK	MILK
DAY 5	MILK	MILK FIRST FRUIT PURÉE (PEAR) *see page 29*	MILK AVOCADO PURÉE *see page 31*	MILK	MILK
DAY 6	MILK	MILK MASHED PAPAYA *see page 29*	MILK CREAMY VEG PURÉE (CARROT) *see page 28*	MILK	MILK
DAY 7	MILK	MILK MASHED BANANA & PAPAYA *see page 29*	MILK FIRST VEG PURÉE (POTATO) *see page 28*	MILK	MILK

MENUS: 6–9 months

YOU CAN NOW OFFER a wider variety of flavours and textures.
Let your baby's appetite guide you as to how much milk
you give with solid meals and whether you give one or
two courses. I have made suggestions for simple desserts
at lunchtime and you can include something similar at
supper if your baby still seems hungry after his main course.

	BREAKFAST	SNACK	LUNCH	SNACK	SUPPER	BEDTIME
DAY 1	MILK CEREAL MASHED BANANA *see page 29*	MILK	POTATO, LEEK & PEA PURÉE *see page 42* JUICE FIRST FRUIT PURÉE (PEAR) *see page 29*	MILK	FISH WITH CARROTS & ORANGE *see page 46*	MILK
DAY 2	MILK DRIED APRICOTS WITH SEMOLINA *see page 42*	MILK	FIRST CHICKEN CASSEROLE *see page 47* JUICE FIRST FRUIT PURÉE (APPLE) *see page 29*	MILK	TOMATO & CAULIFLOWER GRATIN WITH COOKED CARROT STICKS *see page 44*	MILK
DAY 3	MILK CEREAL FIRST FRUIT PURÉE (APPLE & PEAR) *see page 29*	MILK	BRAISED BEEF WITH CARROT, PARSNIP & POTATO *see page 47* FROMAGE FRAIS	MILK	PAPAYA & COTTAGE CHEESE *see page 40*	MILK
DAY 4	MILK WELL COOKED SCRAMBLED EGG WITH TOAST YOGURT	MILK	LENTIL & VEGETABLE PURÉE *see page 43* PEACH PURÉE WITH BABY RICE *see page 31*	MILK	TRIO OF ROOT VEGETABLES *see page 43*	MILK
DAY 5	MILK CEREAL	MILK	PLAICE FILLET WITH LEEK & CHEESE SAUCE *see page 45* PEACH, APPLE & STRAWBERRY PURÉE *see page 41*	MILK	SWEET POTATO, CARROT & BROCCOLI *see page 44*	MILK
DAY 6	MILK APRICOT, PEAR, PEACH & APPLE COMPÔTE *see page 41* FROMAGE FRAIS	MILK	PAPAYA & CHICKEN PURÉE *see page 40* YOGURT	MILK	FILLET OF COD WITH A TRIO OF VEGETABLES *see page 45*	MILK
DAY 7	MILK CEREAL WITH MILK MASHED PAPAYA OR BANANA *see page 29*	MILK	CAULIFLOWER GRATIN (VARIATION) *see page 44* CHUNKS OF SOFT, RIPE FRUIT E.G. PEAR OR PEACH	MILK	SPINACH, POTATO, PARSNIP & LEEK *see page 44*	MILK

MENUS: 9–12 months

MOST OF THESE RECIPES are found in the 9–12 month section, but dishes from previous chapters are also suitable. You can substitute a selection of finger foods, such as strips of roast chicken, cheese, fruit and rice cakes, for cooked meals. Serve the snacks with a drink of milk between main meals, perhaps mid-morning and mid-afternoon.

	BREAKFAST	LUNCH	SUPPER	SNACKS
DAY 1	FRUITY BABY MUESLI *see page 57* YOGURT	QUICK CHICKEN COUSCOUS *see page 60* FRUIT	CHEESY PASTA STARS *see page 58* EXOTIC FRUIT SALAD *see page 57*	MILK SANDWICHES *see page 89* DRIED FRUIT
DAY 2	SCRAMBLED EGG WITH TOAST FIRST FRUIT PURÉE (APPLE) *see page 29*	FILLET OF FISH MORNAY WITH VEGETABLES *see page 59* FRUIT	PASTA WITH TOMATO & MASCARPONE SAUCE *see page 58* FRUIT	MILK VEGETABLE FINGERS AND TOAST STRIPS WITH DIPS YOGURT
DAY 3	CEREAL FRUIT FROMAGE FRAIS	BABY'S BOLOGNESE *see page 61* FRUIT	EASY MASHED VEGETABLE DUO *see page 56* BANANA	MILK SANDWICHES *see page 89* GRATED APPLE
DAY 4	TOAST WITH YEAST EXTRACT OR JAM FRUIT	FLAKED COD WITH TOMATOES & COURGETTES *see page 60* YOGURT	CREAMY CHICKEN & BROCCOLI *see page 61* FRUIT	MILK VEGETABLE FINGERS AND CHEESE STICKS DRIED FRUIT
DAY 5	APPLE & DATE PORRIDGE *see page 57* FRUIT	FRUITY CHICKEN WITH CARROTS *see page 61* FROMAGE FRAIS	CHEESY PASTA STARS *see page 58* APPLE PURÉE *see page 29*	MILK SANDWICHES *see page 89* FRUIT
DAY 6	RAISIN TOAST FINGERS APPLE & PEAR PURÉE *see page 29*	BRAISED BEEF WITH CARROT, PARSNIP & POTATO *see page 47* YOGURT	STEAMED VEGETABLE FINGERS AND CHEESE STICKS FRUIT	MILK CHEESE ON TOAST FRUIT
DAY 7	CEREAL JUICY PEAR & PRUNE PURÉE *see page 41*	CALIFORNIA CHICKEN *see page 60* FRUIT	CAULIFLOWER GRATIN (VARIATION) *see page 44* FRUIT	MILK SANDWICHES *see page 89* YOGURT

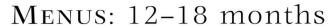

MENUS: 12–18 months

YOUR CHILD is now able to join in family meals and many of these recipes are suitable for the whole family. Choose your preferred accompaniments to main courses, perhaps pasta, potatoes, bread or rice, and a selection of vegetables. Your child should also drink at least 400ml (⅔ pint) of milk daily, which can be given with his snacks.

	BREAKFAST	LUNCH	SUPPER	SNACKS
DAY 1	TOAST WITH YEAST EXTRACT OR JAM YOGURT FRUIT	TURKEY BALLS & PEPPER SAUCE *see page 76* FRUIT	ORZO WITH COLOURFUL DICED VEGETABLES *see page 73* APRICOT & PEAR PURÉE *see page 31*	MILK SANDWICHES *see page 89* YOGURT
DAY 2	CEREAL FROMAGE FRAIS FRUIT	SHEPHERD'S PIE *see page 77* RASPBERRY FROZEN YOGURT *see page 78*	COURGETTE & TOMATO FRITTATA *see page 70* FRUIT	MILK TOASTED HAM AND CHEESE SANDWICH DRIED FRUIT
DAY 3	SCRAMBLED EGG WITH TOAST FRUIT	CHICKEN SAUSAGE SNAIL *see page 75* YOGURT	PASTA CARTWHEELS (VARIATION) *see page 71* BANANA	MILK CREAMY AVOCADO DIP & VEGETABLE FINGERS *see page 56* FRUIT
DAY 4	APRICOT & BLUEBERRY PORRIDGE *see page 70* YOGURT	MINI PIZZA *see page 91* FRUIT SALAD	TUNA & COURGETTE LASAGNE *see page 72* FRUIT	MILK BAKED BEANS WITH TOAST FROMAGE FRAIS AND FRUIT
DAY 5	BOILED EGG WITH FINGERS OF TOAST FROMAGE FRAIS FRUIT	FINGER PICKING CHICKEN & POTATO BALLS *see page 77* BANANA	PASTA WITH TOMATO & MASCARPONE SAUCE *see page 58* FRUIT	MILK VEGETABLE FINGERS AND OTHER FINGER FOODS ICE CREAM
DAY 6	CEREAL YOGURT AND FRUIT	BOW-TIE PASTA WITH HAM & PEAS *see page 73* FRUIT	FRITTATA *see page 70* FRUIT	MILK BAKED BEANS WITH TOAST BANANA
DAY 7	YOGURT PANCAKES WITH MAPLE SYRUP *see page 78* FRUIT	PASTA CARTWHEELS WITH CHEESE & BROCCOLI *see page 71* ICE-CREAM	JOY'S FISH PIE *see page 74* FRUIT	MILK BREAD STICKS WITH CHUNKY TOMATO & CREAM CHEESE DIP *see page 88* DRIED FRUIT

MENUS: 18 months–2 years

SHARED FAMILY MEALS are not always possible, so I have included recipes that can be prepared in advance or frozen so that your toddler can eat the same food as you but at an earlier time. At this age, most children tend not to eat much at one sitting so between-meals snacks with milk are especially important.

	BREAKFAST	LUNCH	SUPPER	SNACKS
DAY 1	CEREAL CHEESE FRUIT	ANNABEL'S VEGETABLE RISSOLES *see page 94* HOMEMADE ICE LOLLIPOP *see page 99*	CHICKEN BOLOGNESE *see page 97* FRUIT	MILK SANDWICHES *see page 89* YOGURT
DAY 2	SCRAMBLED EGG WITH CHEESE & TOMATO *see page 88* FIRST FRUIT PURÉE (APPLE) *see page 29*	BOW-TIE PASTA WITH SPRING VEGETABLES *see page 90* FRUIT	SHEPHERD'S PIE *see page 77* FRUIT	MILK BAKED BEANS WITH TOAST FROMAGE FRAIS
DAY 3	APRICOT & BLUEBERRY PORRIDGE *see page 70* YOGURT	ALPHABET PASTA MINESTRONE *see page 90* FRUIT	SALMON STARFISH *see page 95* FRUIT	MILK CHEESE ON TOAST DRIED FRUIT AND RICE CAKES
DAY 4	CEREAL STRAWBERRY & BANANA SMOOTHIE *see page 98*	LAMB MEATBALLS WITH A SWEET & SOUR SAUCE *see page 97* RASPBERRY FROZEN YOGURT *see page 78*	MULTI-COLOURED RICE WITH KIDNEY BEANS *see page 92* FRUIT	MILK RAISIN & OATMEAL BISCUITS *see page 98* FRUIT
DAY 5	APPLE, MANGO & APRICOT MUESLI *see page 88* YOGURT	MINI PIZZAS *see page 91* JELLY AND ICE-CREAM	CHICKEN KEBABS WITH HONEY & CITRUS MARINADE *see page 96* FRUIT	MILK RAW VEGETABLES AND OTHER FINGER FOODS BANANA MUFFIN *see page 98*
DAY 6	BANANA MUFFIN *see page 98* FROMAGE FRAIS FRUIT	CHICKEN SAUSAGE SNAIL *see page 75* FRUIT	COURGETTE & TOMATO FRITTATA *see page 70* MOCK FRIED EGG MADE WITH VANILLA YOGURT AND APRICOT *see page 103*	MILK SANDWICHES *see page 89* FRUIT
DAY 7	TOAST WITH YEAST EXTRACT OR JAM FRUIT YOGURT AND HONEY	SWEETCORN, CHERRY TOMATO & TOFU KEBAB *see page 92* FRUIT	ONE-POT RICE WITH CHICKEN *see page 96* FRUIT	MILK SARDINES ON TOAST STRAWBERRY & BANANA SMOOTHIE *see page 98*

MENUS: 2–3 years

THIS MENU PLAN shows a progressively wider choice of recipes that will accustom your child to new tastes. As with the other menu charts, you can substitute a few healthy convenience foods, such as pizzas, cooked chicken pieces or fish fingers, and vary or omit desserts, but do aim to keep snacks nutritious and provide milk, fruit juice or water.

	BREAKFAST	LUNCH	SUPPER	SNACKS
DAY 1	APPLE, MANGO & APRICOT MUESLI *see page 88* YOGURT AND HONEY	PASTA WITH COURGETTES, PEPPERS & SAUSAGES *see page 109* FRUIT AND ICE-CREAM	TERIYAKI CHICKEN STIR-FRY *see page 111* FROMAGE FRAIS	MILK SANDWICHES *see page 89* FRUIT
DAY 2	BOILED EGG WITH FINGERS OF TOAST FRUIT FROMAGE FRAIS	TOMATO SOUP *see page 106* FRUIT	ANNABEL'S TASTY MEATBALLS *see page 112* ICE-CREAM	MILK BANANA MUFFIN *see page 98* NATURAL YOGURT AND HONEY
DAY 3	CEREAL CHEESE FRUIT	BOW-TIE PASTA WITH HAM & PEAS *see page 73* SALAD JELLY AND ICE-CREAM	VEGETABLE LASAGNE *see page 109* FRUIT	MILK BAKED BEANS WITH TOAST FRUIT
DAY 4	PORRIDGE RAISIN TOAST FRUIT	ANNABEL'S VEGETABLE RISSOLES *see page 94* STICKY TOFFEE PUDDING *see page 113*	GOLDEN TURKEY FINGERS *see page 110* YOGURT	MILK CHEESE AND VEGETABLE STICKS FRUIT
DAY 5	TOAST WITH YEAST EXTRACT OR JAM YOGURT FRUIT	HEART-SHAPED CHICKEN NUGGETS *see page 110* FRUIT	ANNABEL'S PASTA SALAD *see page 108* RAW VEGETABLES & DIP ICE-CREAM	MILK RAISIN & OATMEAL BISCUIT *see page 98* CHOCOLATE SMOOTHIE *see page 98*
DAY 6	CEREAL YOGURT FRUIT	GOLDEN TURKEY FINGERS *see page 110* RAISIN & OATMEAL BISCUITS *see page 98*	HUNGARIAN GOULASH *see page 112* FRUIT	MILK CHEESE ON TOAST DRIED FRUIT
DAY 7	SCRAMBLED EGG WITH TOAST FRUIT	CARAMELISED CHICKEN BREAST *see page 110* FRUIT	MINI BAKED POTATO *see page 107* SALAD FRUIT	MILK SANDWICHES *see page 89* HOMEMADE ICE LOLLIPOP *see page 99*

MENUS: 3–5 years

AT THIS AGE, children love to help prepare their meals and there are many simple things they can do, like cut sandwich shapes. Although I have suggested fruit after most meals, it is fine to offer occasional treats like cheesecake or trifle. If your child eats lunch at nursery or pre-school, just balance her evening meal at home accordingly.

	BREAKFAST	LUNCH	SUPPER	SNACKS
DAY 1	POACHED OR FRIED EGG WITH FINGERS OF TOAST CEREAL FRUIT	SPAGHETTI WITH SPECIAL TOMATO SAUCE *see page 122* SALAD YOGURT	PAELLA *see page 126* FRUIT	MILK VEGETABLE STICKS WITH HUMMOUS BANANA MUFFIN *see page 98*
DAY 2	APPLE, MANGO & APRICOT MUESLI *see page 88* YOGURT FRUIT	BEEF TERIYAKI SKEWERS *see page 129* SALAD FRUIT	ITALIAN RISOTTO WITH MUSHROOMS & PEAS *see page 123* ICE-CREAM FRUIT	MILK CHEESE ON TOAST CHEWY APRICOT & CEREAL BAR *see page 131*
DAY 3	PORRIDGE WITH HONEY OR JAM THINLY SLICED CHEESE OR MINIATURE CHEESES FRUIT	STICKY BAR-B-Q DRUMSTICKS *see page 126* RASPBERRY FROZEN YOGURT *see page 78*	SINGAPORE NOODLES *see page 128* EXOTIC FRUIT SALAD *see page 57*	MILK BAKED BEANS WITH TOAST CHOCOLATE CHIP & ORANGE CUT-OUT COOKIES *see page 130*
DAY 4	SCRAMBLED EGG WITH CHEESE & TOMATO *see page 88* TOAST FRUIT	CHICKEN SATAY *see page 127* FRUIT	FISH & OVEN-BAKED CHIPS *see page 125* JELLY AND ICE-CREAM	MILK SANDWICHES *see page 89* FRUIT
DAY 5	YOGURT PANCAKES WITH MAPLE SYRUP *see page 78* FROMAGE FRAIS FRUIT	MINI BAKED POTATOES *see page 107* FRUIT	BEEF STIR-FRY WITH OYSTER SAUCE *see page 128* STICKY TOFFEE PUDDING *see page 113*	MILK VEGETABLE AND CHEESE STICKS RAISIN & OATMEAL BISCUITS *see page 98*
DAY 6	CEREAL CHEESE FRUIT	MINI BEAN & VEGGIE ENCHILADAS *see page 125* FRUIT	CHICKEN BOLOGNESE *see page 97* JELLY & ICE-CREAM	MILK SANDWICHES *see page 89* DRIED FRUIT FROMAGE FRAIS
DAY 7	WAFFLE & MAPLE SYRUP FRUIT YOGURT	EGG-FRIED RICE WITH CHICKEN & PRAWNS *see page 127*	MILDLY SPICED VEGETABLE SAMOSAS *see page 124* FRUIT	MILK COUNTRY APPLE CAKE *see page 130* FRUIT

Snacks & Party Food

SNACKS FORM AN IMPORTANT part of young children's diet. Encourage them to eat healthily now and you will lay the foundation for a lifetime of healthy eating. For special meals, such as a birthday tea, you could make up an individual picnic box for each child rather than laying a table.

HEALTHY SNACKS

RECIPES FOR SNACKS

STRAWBERRY & BANANA SMOOTHIE
see page 98

CHUNKY TOMATO
& CREAM CHEESE DIP/CREAMY AVOCADO
DIP & VEGETABLE FINGERS
see pages 88 and 56

MOCK FRIED EGG
(VANILLA YOGURT & TINNED PEACH HALF)
see page 103

RAISIN & OATMEAL BISCUITS
see page 98

BANANA MUFFINS
see page 98

HOMEMADE ICE LOLLIPOPS
see page 99

RASPBERRY FROZEN YOGURT
see page 78

ROOT VEGETABLE CHIPS
see page 70

SANDWICHES
see page 89

SCRAMBLED EGGS WITH CHEESE & TOMATO
see page 88

MIXED SALAD WITH DRESSING FROM
ANNABEL'S PASTA SALAD
see page 108

OTHER IDEAS

BOILED EGG WITH FINGERS OF TOAST; FRENCH BREAD;
CHEESE ON TOAST; TOASTED RAISIN BREAD
FINGERS WITH CREAM CHEESE; TOASTED SANDWICHES
(E.G. HAM & CHEESE); MINIATURE CHEESES & CHEESE SLICES;
DRIED FRUIT; FRESH FRUIT & FRUIT SALAD;
WHOLEGRAIN BREAKFAST CEREAL WITH MILK; BAKED
BEANS ON TOAST; GLASS OF MILK OR FRESH ORANGE JUICE;
POPCORN; YOGURT; RICE CAKES; CRISPBREADS;
BREAD STICKS; VEGETABLES (E.G. CARROTS, CUCUMBER,
CHERRY TOMATOES, CELERY, ON THEIR OWN OR WITH A DIP)

PARTY PLANNER

PREPARE IN ADVANCE

PARCEL BIRTHDAY CAKE
see page 115

HEART-SHAPED CHICKEN NUGGETS
see page 110

CHUNKY TOMATO & CREAM CHEESE DIP
(CUT CRUDITÉS THE DAY BEFORE THE PARTY)
see page 88

CHARACTER FAIRY CAKES
(DECORATE THE DAY BEFORE THE PARTY)
see page 114

CHOCOLATE CHOUX PASTRY MICE
(DECORATE THE DAY BEFORE THE PARTY)
see page 131

CHEWY APRICOT & CEREAL BARS
see page 131

JELLY BOATS
(CUT IN HALF & DECORATE ON THE DAY)
see page 79

SHORTBREAD COOKIES
see page 115

MAKE ON THE DAY

SANDWICH SELECTION
see page 89

ANNABEL'S PASTA SALAD
see page 108

CHICKEN KEBABS
WITH HONEY & CITRUS MARINADE
see page 96

CHICKEN SATAY
see page 127

PASTA WITH
COURGETTES, PEPPERS & SAUSAGES
see page 109

GOLDEN TURKEY FINGERS
see page 110

MINI PIZZAS
see page 91

FRESH FRUIT PLATTER
WITH CHOCOLATE-DIPPED FRUIT

Index

Bold type indicates illustration

Acknowledgments

Author's Acknowledgments

I am indebted to the following people for their help and advice during the writing of this book: Dr. Margaret Lawson, Senior Lecturer in Paediatric Nutrition, Institute of Child Health; Dr. Stephen Herman FRCP, Consultant Paediatrician, Central Middlesex Hospital; Dr. Barry Lewis FRCP, FRCPH Consultant Paediatrician; Luci Daniels, State Registered Dietician; Simon Karmel; David Karmel; Evelyn Etkind; Jane Hamilton; Marian Magpoc; Letty Catada; Jo Pratt; Joy Skipper; Jacqui Morley; Lara Tankel. I would especially like to thank Nicholas, Lara and Scarlett Karmel, and all the other discerning young tasters who have eaten their way through the recipes in this book. Thanks also to photographer Ian O'Leary, and the members of the DK team who have worked on this production.

Dorling Kindersley would like to thank: Dr. Margaret Lawson for advice on nutrition; Jasmine Challis for the nutritional analyses; Dave King for additional photography; Emma Brogi for photographic assistance; Sue Henderson for food styling on pages 86–7; Hilary Bird for the index.

Many thanks to all our models:
Connor Bailey; Sam Bower; Nicoletta Comand and Melisande Croft; Laurie Claxton; Sophie Crook; Liam and Katie Dalmon; Page Fairclough (Bubblegum Agency); Abigail and Matthew Freathy; Harriet Hayles (Bubblegum Agency); Rosie Johnson; Scarlett Karmel; Alexander and Charlotte Kay; Peter Kelleher; Iris Mathieson; Georgina and Jack McCooke; Max Moore; Eleni Neophitou; Elicia Oliver-Knox; Elise Palmer; Kyle Perry; Joshua Richardson; Holly and Claire Robinson; Ellie-Louise Thomson.

Photography credits Recipe photography by Ian O'Leary, except pp. 86-7 by Dave King. Other food photography by Ian O'Leary, Andy Crawford, Clive Streeter and Dave King.
Model photography by Andy Crawford, except pp.9–11 by Steve Gorton; p.15, tl, p.67 and p.82, tr, Dave King; p.15, tr, Steve Shott; page 22, bl, Jenny Matthews; p.24, br, Susanna Price; p. 32 and p.33, tr, Julie Fisher; p.34, tr, p.52, bl, p.64, tl, and p.33, tl, Jo Foord.

Useful Addresses

Action Against Allergy
PO Box 278,
Twickenham,
Middlesex TW1 4QQ
No telephone enquiries;
send a SAE for leaflets

The Anaphylaxis Campaign
PO Box 149,
Fleet,
Hampshire GU13 9XU
Tel: 01252–542029

British Dietetic Association
7th Floor, Elizabeth House,
22 Suffolk Street,
Birmingham B1 1LS
Tel: 0121–643 5483

The Coeliac Society
PO Box 220,
High Wycombe,
Buckinghamshire HP11 2HY

The Food Commission
94 White Lion Street,
Islington,
London N1 9PF
Tel: 0171–837 2250
Publishers of *The Food Magazine*

The Vegetarian Society
Parkdale, Dunham Road,
Altrincham,
Cheshire WA14 4QG
Tel: 0161–928 0793
Send a SAE for leaflets

Cooking for Children
49 Berkeley Square
London W1X 5DB
Tel: 0171 355 4555

Lakeland Limited
Alexandra Buildings,
Windermere,
Cumbria LA23 1BQ
Tel: 01539–488200
Kitchen equipment suppliers

Squire's Kitchen
3 Waverley Lane,
Farnham,
Surrey GU9 8BB
Tel: 01252–711749
Icing equipment, food colours